WITHDRAWN

3 SOIS 00000 0001

B
3376
.W564
B37

Bartley, William W.
Wittgenstein

## DATE DUE

| JUN 11 '90 | | | |
|---|---|---|---|
| APR 18 '91 | | | |
| MAY 0 6 1999 | | | |
| | | | |
| | | | |
| | | | |
| | | | |
| | | | |

BRADNER LIBRARY
SCHOOLCRAFT COLLEGE
LIVONIA, MICHIGAN 48152

This is a volume in a new series of PORTRAITS, devoted to figures who have changed the world we live in. The series is edited by Walter Kaufmann, Professor of Philosophy at Princeton University.

The first three volumes are:
    SARTRE *by Hazel E. Barnes*
    WITTGENSTEIN *by William Warren Bartley III*
    LENIN *by Rolf H. W. Theen*

They will soon be followed by:
    LUTHER *by Richard Marius*
    ENGELS *by Alfred Meyer*
    LINCOLN *by Hans Morgenthau*

*William Warren Bartley III*

# WITTGENSTEIN

𝍖 𝍖 𝍖 𝍖 𝍖

## J. B. LIPPINCOTT COMPANY

*Philadelphia and New York*

Copyright © 1973 by William Warren Bartley III
All rights reserved
First edition
Printed in the United States of America
Book design by Adrianne Onderdonk Dudden

*193*

*W 831 B 6*

FRONTISPIECE: *Wittgenstein as an Austrian army officer,
from his Army Identity Card, June 30, 1918.*

The photographs in this book are reproduced with the kind
permission of Rudolf Koder.

*B
3376
.W564
B37*

U.S. Library of Congress Cataloging in Publication Data

Bartley, William Warren, birth date
    Wittgenstein.

    (Portraits)
    "Works by Wittgenstein": p.
    1. Wittgenstein, Ludwig, 1889–1951.
B3376.W564B37      192 [B]      72–11755
ISBN–0–397–00751–5

*To the memory of my father*
*1895–1967*

# CONTENTS

回 回 回

Photographs appear on pages 4, 49, 131, and 151.

# EDITOR'S PREFACE

回 回 回

It has been said that every great philosopher has given philosophy a new direction, but that only Wittgenstein has done this twice—first with his *Tractatus*, published right after World War I, and then again with the ideas that found their final form in his *Philosophical Investigations*, published posthumously after World War II. The early work influenced logical positivism, the later work the analytical philosophy that flourished in the English-speaking world for roughly a quarter of a century. No other philosopher has had nearly so great an influence on twentieth-century Anglo-American philosophy. Yet Wittgenstein was an Austrian who wrote his books in German. His life and personality were enigmatic —especially the decisive years during which he developed his later philosophy.

Knowing of W. W. Bartley's researches concerning the "lost" years in Wittgenstein's life, I invited him to write this book. I had no doubt that it would be interesting and important, but did not foresee the extent of Bartley's discoveries, which may strike some readers as sensational. Right from the start, we are swept up in the excitement of the author's quest for the man who, having published a book that made history, went on to teach at primary schools in two small Austrian villages while he changed his mind about many of his most influential ideas. The portrait that emerges from this account is human—all too human—but the author's respect for Wittgenstein is never in doubt. Though brief and written so that it can be understood by those with no previous knowledge of Wittgenstein's philosophy, this book is an important contribution to our understanding of the man and of the development of his thought.

Actually, I do not believe that every great philosopher has given philosophy a new direction. This one-dimensional metaphor gives us no idea of Plato's or Aristotle's importance, or of the significance of Spinoza, Hegel, or Nietzsche. If a philosopher's ideas are promptly taken up by a school and developed only in one direction, this may well point to a lack of richness, of dimension, of profundity. It may be a mark of greatness in a philosopher if he feels distressed by his influence—as Wittgenstein did. He was not only one of the most influential philosophers of his century but also one of the most remarkable men of our time. Bartley does not see him merely as a link in a chain, nor does he concentrate on the human being to the exclusion of his thought. What he offers us is a concise intellectual biography of an extraordinary man.

WALTER KAUFMANN

# ACKNOWLEDGMENTS

回 回 回

The help of the following persons has been invaluable. Needless to say, they are in no way responsible for my conclusions and have in several cases disagreed with them. I am also indebted to several persons who, for reasons of their own, do not wish their names to be mentioned. My most sincere thanks go to:

Professor Joseph Agassi, Frau Dir. Georg Berger, Frau Margarete Bicklmayer, Professor I. M. Bochenski, Herr Franz Brenner, Professor Sylvain Bromberger, Professor Charlotte Bühler, the late Professor Rudolf Carnap, Professor R. S. Cohen, Frau Anny Eder, Professor Herbert Feigl, Professor Paul K. Feyerabend, Herr Karl Gruber, Herr und Frau Konrad Gruber, Frau L. Hausmann, Professor F. A. von Hayek, Dr. W. D. Hudson, Dr. Hanns Jäger, Professor Bernard Kaplan, Herr Helmut Kasper, Herr und Frau Rudolf Koder, Herr Bürgermeister Emmerich Koderhold, Professor Viktor Kraft, Professor Laurens Laudan, Mr. Michael Lebeck, Frau Gerda Leber-Hagenau, Dr. Gustav Lebzeltern, Dr. F. Lenz, Mr. Wallace Nethery, Professor George Pitcher, Dr. Günter Posch, Mr. Dolf Rijkers, Herr Norbert Rosner, Herr Johann Scheibenbauer, Herr Dir. Martin Scherleitner, Professor Herbert Spiegelberg, Dr. Thomas H. W. Stonborough, Dr. George Steiner, Professor Marx Wartofsky, Professor Albert Wellek, Professor J. O. Wisdom.

I am also indebted to the staff of the following institutions for their cooperation and help: Landesarchiv für Niederösterreich, Vienna; Stadtbibliothek, Vienna; Kriegsarchiv, Staatsarchiv, Vienna; Pädagogisches Institut der Stadt Wien; Pädagogisches Zentralbücherei, Vienna; Stadtschulrat für Wien, Vienna; Stadtarchiv, Bielefeld; Stadtarchiv, Korbach.

I am deeply indebted to the Research Committees of the University of Pittsburgh; of Gonville and Caius College, Cambridge; and of the University of California, which at various times supported my investigations into German and Austrian intellectual history.

Above all I am indebted to Walter Kaufmann—for his inspiration as well as for his radical yet constructive criticism of the manuscript of this work.

# INTRODUCTION

◨ ◨ ◨

*But I say unto you, That every idle word that men shall speak, they shall give account thereof in the day of judgment. For by thy words thou shalt be justified, and by thy words thou shalt be condemned.*

—*Matthew 12:36–37*

## I

Ludwig Wittgenstein was born in Vienna in 1889 and died in Cambridge, England, in 1951. He was one of the half-dozen most influential philosophers of this century.

My presentation of his philosophy spans both his early and his later thought—the ideas of the *Tractatus Logico-Philosophicus* (1921 and 1922) as well as those developed in the posthumously published work, most importantly *Philosophical Investigations*. The biographical focus of the essay is much more restricted. I have seen no point in repeating well-known stories of Wittgenstein's life in Vienna, Manchester and Cambridge before the First World War or after his return to professional philosophical activity in 1929. Rather, I have concentrated on the decade in his life following the First War. These are mystery years about which little has been written. I emphasize them here for two reasons: I may have something new to say about them which will contribute to a better understanding of Wittgenstein; and I happen to believe that this transitional period is in many ways the most important of his life.

Since the study contains new information about Wittgenstein's development in the twenties that throws light on his later concerns, it will interest specialists. But I have tried to set down my account in such a way that readers who are not philosophers will be able to understand it too.

Thus I should report that the man with whom we are concerned was born into one of the most eminent families of Vienna's haute bourgeoisie. He was the youngest of seven children born to Karl Wittgenstein, creator of Austria's prewar iron and steel industry and a great patron of culture, particularly of the visual arts and of music. As a child Ludwig was educated by private tutors, but when an adolescent he was sent to secondary school in Linz. His ambition at that time was to become an engineer like his father, and in 1906 he enrolled in the Technische Hochschule in Berlin-Charlottenburg, where he spent three semesters. In 1908 he went to England to continue his engineering studies at Manchester University, where he did pioneering work in aeronautics. His mathematical work in engineering aroused his interest in the foundations of mathematics and in logic, and in 1911, on the advice of the great German logician Gottlob Frege (1848–1925), he went to Cambridge to study philosophy with Bertrand Russell. During the two years following, he made a dazzlingly brilliant impression in Cambridge, gained the friendship of two of that University's most distinguished philosophers, G. E. Moore and Russell, and was elected to that most select of secret societies, The Apostles, to which Moore, Russell and most of the male members of the Bloomsbury group already belonged.

Wittgenstein spent the year immediately prior to the outbreak of the First World War in seclusion in Norway, working at logic in a hut he built for himself. When the war began, he volunteered for the Austrian Army, where in due course he became an officer. During the war he completed the manuscript of a short philosophical work, *Tractatus Logico-Philosophicus*, now regarded as one of the greatest philosophical achievements of this century.

After the war he turned away from philosophy for a time: he took odd jobs as a gardener and hotel porter and spent six years as an elementary schoolteacher in lower Austria. During the late twenties his interest in professional philosophy was rekindled, partly as a result of his friendship with Moritz Schlick, leader of the Vienna Circle, and in 1929 he returned to Cambridge, where he was soon awarded the doctorate and elected Fellow of Trinity College. In 1939 he succeeded Moore as Professor of Philosophy at Cambridge, and held his chair—with interruptions for civilian war service (as hospital orderly and laboratory technician) in Britain—until 1947, when he retired to devote more time to writing.

Although he wrote voluminously, the only philosophical work to be published in his lifetime was the *Tractatus* (1922) and a brief article in the *Proceedings of the Aristotelian Society*. His literary executors have been publishing his other philosophical writings posthumously. The most important, *Philosophical Investigations*, was published in 1953.

In appearance, Wittgenstein was of medium height, slender, with blue eyes and fair hair. His piercing glance and intense concentration, combined with fantastic presence, gave him a most unusual charismatic quality which attracted fanatically devoted and loyal students to his side. By the mid-1930s he had succeeded, through teaching rather than publication, in forming a strong and brilliant group of disciples.

Wittgenstein was baptized in the Roman Catholic faith and was given a Roman Catholic burial. Although his father and grandfather were prominent Viennese Protestants, his mother was Roman Catholic, and until the end of his First World War army duty he continued to give his own religion as "Roman Catholic." In later years, while stating firmly that he was not an adherent to any organized religion, he nonetheless observed the rituals of organized religions when he encountered them. He avoided criticizing the Church and its clergy, had good friends among the clergy, and seriously contemplated entering monastic life himself. Some of his closest friends in Vienna were devout Roman Catholics, as were several of his favorite students in Cambridge. By descent, as opposed to persuasion, Wittgenstein was partly Jewish. Outside the family the descent was not widely known; the matter is taken up briefly in an addendum at the back of this book.

## II

Wittgenstein insisted that philosophical encounter with him produce moral change. In a moving part of his memoir of Wittgenstein, his student Norman Malcolm reports how bitterly Wittgenstein complained when this did not happen: "What is the use of studying philosophy," Wittgenstein asked, "if all that it does for you is to enable you to talk with some plausibility about some abstruse questions of logic, etc., & if it does not improve your thinking about the important questions of everyday life?" [1]

My own interest in Wittgenstein was awakened when I discovered that this man had actually gone about practicing what he preached—or, to be more accurate, had practiced what he once wrote could not be said but only shown. I had had the good luck, during the course of an as yet uncompleted investigation into central European intellectual life following the collapse of the Hapsburg monarchy, to stumble upon material about the dark decade in Wittgenstein's life from the end of the First World War until his return to Cambridge in 1929. I learned some of the details of his life, of his personal and intellectual milieux, during his years as an elementary schoolteacher in three tiny mountain villages in lower Austria. As details and anecdotes hitherto disconnected and unexplained gradually fell into place, an altogether startling image emerged of a man who had, contrary to all accounts, *not* abandoned philosophy at all after the First World War and the publication of the *Tractatus*, but who was, rather, attempting to put into practice the ethical portion of his earlier philosophy and at the same time beginning to formulate the concerns that were to dominate his later philosophy.

I was led to the material just mentioned in a roundabout way. In the course of my research I had come

[1] Norman Malcolm, *Ludwig Wittgenstein: A Memoir* (London: Oxford University Press, 1966), p. 39.

upon some knowledge of two related topics: Otto Glöckel's school-reform movement, now almost totally forgotten even in Austria, and the philosophical and psychological ideas of Karl Bühler. Bühler is hardly forgotten; indeed, a mild revival of interest in his work has begun in recent years. Still, few English or American psychologists know much about his work, and he died in comparative obscurity in Los Angeles in 1963. In the twenties and thirties, however, he had been world famous as one of the greatest psychologists of Europe and a leading figure of the first Austrian Republic.

Certain similarities between some of the themes of Glöckel's program and Bühler's theories on the one hand, and ideas which infuse the later work of Wittgenstein on the other, caused me to recall dimly that Wittgenstein had taught elementary school in Austria in the twenties, and to wonder whether there might not be some connection. As it turned out, the connection was quite direct.

But when I began my work, the idea that there was any link between Glöckel, Bühler, and Wittgenstein was no more than the shakiest of hunches. So it was with some diffidence that I rented a car in Vienna one summer weekday morning for the long, and I feared unprofitable, drive to the remote villages of Trattenbach, Otterthal and Puchberg, in the part of lower Austria known as Semmering or Neunkirchen, where Wittgenstein had taught from 1920 to 1926. I had no reason to suppose that anyone would remember him. Indeed, would any of the present inhabitants of these villages ever have known him? Trattenbach and Otterthal had, I had learned, been on the Russian front during the Second World War. And if anyone did remember Wittgenstein, would he or she talk about him? This part of Austria is not tourist country, and its peasants are sometimes suspicious and taciturn.

In the event, I did reach both Trattenbach and Otterthal that day; they are only about three miles apart and were until 1923 part of the same administrative community. But Puchberg had to be set aside for later visits —Trattenbach and Otterthal alone were to occupy me for weeks.

After the long climb into the hills above Gloggnitz, I pulled up to have lunch at one of the three simple inns in Otterthal. I had armed myself with the paperback edition of Malcolm's memoir of Wittgenstein, with its photo on the cover to jog failing memories, and also with a copy of Wittgenstein's letters to his friend Paul Engelmann, where Wittgenstein's German original faces the English translation, and the villages are mentioned by name. So I could if necessary prove to doubters that such a man really had lived in these places. As I finished my tea, I began to look around for someone old enough to have been one of Wittgenstein's pupils, someone in his or her late fifties or early sixties. In a corner of the restaurant an old peasant woman with a bun of white hair, clad in a black dress, was busily scrubbing the floor. So I stepped over to her to ask if she might happen to remember anyone named Wittgenstein, or anyone who might have known him. I expected a bewildered apology; instead I got an explosive: "Wittgenstein! *Ludwig* Wittgenstein? Der Lehrer! Ach, freilich!" ("The teacher! Well, of course!").

The old woman asked me how he was—it turned out

that she was in her early seventies—and I had to report that he had died in 1951. Not quite knowing where to begin, I pulled out Malcolm and Engelmann. The photo she declared a good likeness, while remarking that she hadn't, of course, seen him since 1926: "The trial, you know." Actually, I didn't know, but that was only one of the things I began to learn about that afternoon. Just about everyone in Trattenbach and Otterthal "knew about" Ludwig Wittgenstein (although they did not, except in one or two cases, know that he had "gone on" to become a philosopher), and many who had been his students, or whose brothers and sisters had attended his classes, still lived there.

The central part of Otterthal consists of little more than a crossroads lined by small farmhouses. It was extraordinary to walk down the main road, calling out to peasants working in their gardens or sitting on their porches, and being given details in the most matter-of-fact way about a man whose name I had hitherto encountered only in books or in the conversation of philosophers and intellectuals. The remarks of these people, who knew nothing of Wittgenstein's philosophy and next to nothing of his later fame, convinced me that Ludwig Wittgenstein had been truly extraordinary.

Several hours after that first lunch I drove three miles westward down the road to Trattenbach. By then I knew that I would have to spend many days in these villages, despite my intention to do no more than look them over and take a few photographs before driving back to Vienna. I parked in front of a small general store not far from the village center and wandered in to buy some bananas. As I counted out the few schillings to the grocer I asked—by now routinely—whether he remembered a schoolteacher named Wittgenstein. The grocer stared at me, called for his wife to take over the store, and led me to a chair in the back room. Of course he remembered Wittgenstein: Wittgenstein had lived upstairs, in the attic of that grocery store, for nearly a year; and this grocer, Johann Scheibenbauer, had been one of his students from 1920 to 1922. It was strange, he remarked, that I had just bought bananas from him, for Ludwig Wittgenstein had given him *his* first banana—and his first orange—in those bleak postwar years when German Austria was starving. In order to feed his students, Wittgenstein had climbed for miles with packages of fruit bundled in a large knapsack on his back. In those days there was no public transportation to Trattenbach and Otterthal; those who went there hiked over twelve miles uphill through the forest from the train station at Gloggnitz, just as Wittgenstein had done.

Night had fallen before I was to take leave of Herr Scheibenbauer and those of his friends whom he had called in, in order to drive back to Vienna and make preparations for further trips and a longer stay in these villages.

## III

An ulterior motive for focusing on a wholly Austrian decade in Wittgenstein's life (a decade during which he left Austria only four times—once for a two-week trip to Holland and northern Germany, once for a brief summer trip to England after an absence of over twelve years, and twice to work or holiday in Norway) is to remind those who have come to view Wittgenstein as a very English figure that in fact every decade in his life was an Austrian one, save that period of some nine years immediately before, during and after the Second World War when he was forced by circumstances quite beyond his control to remain in Britain. Any person who might be surprised by this statement would do well to reflect that the three Cambridge academic full terms are after all only eight weeks each in length, that Wittgenstein rarely arrived or lingered in Cambridge more than a few days before and after term, and that it was his habit, even in some of his most active Cambridge years, to spend twenty-five or twenty-six weeks each year in Vienna or on one of the family estates, such as the Hochreit, the country seat near Hohenberg in lower Austria that his father had bought in 1894.

If one accepts that the ways in which one styles oneself—the games one plays with one's own name—say a lot about who one is or would like to be, then how revealing it is to find out that Ludwig Wittgenstein characterized himself in the *Wiener Adreßbuch,* the Viennese City Directory, in each edition from 1933 to 1938, as "Dr. Ludwig Wittgenstein, occupation: *architect,*" a resident of Vienna, living, together with his sister Hermine and brother Paul at the Palais Wittgenstein, Argentinierstraße 16. I had often heard of his schemes to become a monk, an architect, or an orchestral conductor but had hardly known how seriously to take them. Here is tangible evidence of Wittgenstein's ambivalence about his English academic attachments even during the very peak of his professional attainment in Cambridge.

Wittgenstein first went to Britain in 1908 and died there forty-three years later, a few days after his sixty-second birthday. Between 1908 and 1937 he spent a total of only about seven and one half years in England; from 1938 to 1946 he spent nine years there; from the beginning of 1947 until his death he was to spend only around twenty-one months on English soil.

Wittgenstein was not, then, one of those German-speaking intellectuals who emigrated from Germany or Austria when comparatively young and *settled* in one of the English-speaking countries. Because so many such persons exist who left Germany during the political and economic upheavals of the 1920s and 1930s, students are prone to classify Wittgenstein with these émigrés, with such persons as Rudolf Carnap and Herbert Feigl in America or Friedrich Waismann in England. Wittgenstein was of an earlier generation and a different class, a member of the pre-First World War international haute bourgeoisie. Nor was English a language that he had to acquire as an adult; he grew up, like many other members of his class and others of his family, speaking fluent English and French as well as German.

In my research for this essay I have, therefore, drawn principally on Austrian resources, on archives and on people. In Vienna as well as in lower Austria I searched out Wittgenstein's former students; I tracked down the boy—now a widower in his middle sixties—whom Wittgenstein had tried hard to adopt in 1922. I had the pleasure of rounding up for an evening meal in a back room of a decrepit inn in Trattenbach most of Wittgenstein's living elementary school students there. It was during that evening reunion, in the midsummer of 1969, that one of Wittgenstein's old students, a peasant who had had no schooling since Wittgenstein had departed from Trattenbach in 1922, leaned across the table to say: "You know, there was an interesting thing that Lehrer Wittgenstein used to tell us about." And then out came the paradox of the liar![2] I have also talked with members of Wittgenstein's family and with other persons of exceptionally high culture in Vienna who had known Wittgenstein in one way or another. And I have gone to homosexual bars in Vienna and London in search of those who knew Wittgenstein in another way; and I was successful. Some of the material gleaned from these encounters will be reported in the pages that follow. I have also consulted many persons in England and America, but I have deliberately refrained from consulting those who control the Wittgenstein archives, in order that this work be as independent as possible.

I hope that from my footwork—combing the streets of the third district in Vienna, walking alone and rather apprehensively through the Prater late at night, trudging the dusty roads near Hütteldorf and in Neunkirchen, talking with those who remembered Wittgenstein, whether a toothless old school director in his attic room or some aging homosexual in his own special pub—there will emerge a somewhat more vivid picture of this period in the life of an extraordinary philosopher.

I could not begin to list the names of all who have aided me. Most of those who were especially helpful are named in the Acknowledgments. Any reader of the first chapter will understand without further ado why a few persons to whom I am deeply indebted asked that their

[2] See Chapter 2, Section VII below.

names not be revealed. Those who are named have sometimes disagreed with my conclusions. Here I wish to thank only my friend Walter Kaufmann, without whose encouragement and support I would never have published this essay.

WILLIAM WARREN BARTLEY III

Schenley Heights
Pittsburgh
29 April 1971

# WITTGENSTEIN

# 1

## THE MAGIC CARPET

🔲 🔲 🔲

*Whenever you are preoccupied with something, with some trouble or with some problem which is a big thing in your life— as sex is, for instance—then no matter what you start from, the association will lead finally and inevitably back to that same theme. Freud remarks on how, after the analysis of it, the dream appears so very logical. And of course it does. . . . An "Urszene" . . . often has the attractiveness of giving a sort of tragic pattern to one's life. It is all the repetition of the same pattern which was settled long ago. Like a tragic figure carrying out the decrees under which the fates had placed him at birth. Many people have, at some period, serious trouble in their lives—so serious as to lead to thoughts of suicide. This is likely to appear to one as something nasty, as a situation which is too foul to be a subject of a tragedy. And it may then be an immense relief if it can be shown that one's life has the pattern rather of a tragedy—the tragic working out and repetition of a pattern.*

—Ludwig Wittgenstein [1]

### I

One night in the early winter months of 1919, Ludwig Wittgenstein lay sleeping in Monte Cassino, in the camp north of Naples where he spent nine months as a prisoner of war following the fall of the Austro-Hungarian Monarchy. He dreamt as follows:

[1] Transcribed in *Lectures and Conversations on Aesthetics, Psychology and Religious Belief*, compiled from notes taken by Yorick Smythies, Rush Rhees and James Taylor, ed. Cyril Barrett (Berkeley: University of California Press, 1967), pp. 50–51.

It was night. I was outside a house whose windows blazed with light. I went up to a window to look inside. There, on the floor, I noticed an exquisitely beautiful prayer rug, one which I immediately wanted to examine. I tried to open the front door, but a snake darted out to prevent me from entering; I tried another door, but there too a snake darted out to block my way. Snakes appeared also at the windows, and blocked my every effort to reach the prayer rug.

Wittgenstein awoke, and later referred to this as "the first dream." [2]

Wittgenstein had at that time read only a little Freud and was not to begin to read Freud with any care until later that year, after his return to Vienna. But his immediate interpretation of his own dream was straightforward and Freudian. The prayer rug, so he thought, symbolized that for which he had sought for years in vain and for which he was to continue to search for most of the rest of his life: an integration of his libido, a sublimation, for intellectual and spiritual purposes, of his sexual drives. For what does a prayer rug look like? Its central feature is a form rather like that of an erect penis. But this tremendous energy, transformed into a work of art, is *contained* within strong and beautiful borders. Wittgenstein's own situation was not that depicted by the rug-mandala, that goal for which he searched. Rather, at that time his own spiritual progress was checked and thwarted by the loose, ugly, *uncontained*

[2] Unless otherwise indicated, my information is based on conversations and other communications with friends of Wittgenstein's, as explained in the Introduction and the Acknowledgments.

serpents which haunted both his waking and his dreaming hours.

The dream also commented on the ironic contrast between the public and the private Wittgenstein. Already in 1919, long before the publication of his *Tractatus Logico-Philosophicus*, Ludwig Wittgenstein was considered by many to be the finest philosophic talent of his generation; and today many still consider him the greatest philosopher of his time. He was, so his teacher and friend Bertrand Russell wrote, "perhaps the most perfect example I have ever known of genius as traditionally conceived, passionate, profound, intense, and dominating. He had a kind of purity which I have never known equalled except by G. E. Moore." [8] Yet this pure and intense genius who himself wrote that he would like to die in a moment of brilliance [4] was also a homosexual given to bouts of extravagant and almost uncontrollable promiscuity.

Throughout his life, but especially during and following the First World War, Wittgenstein was tormented by intense guilt and suffering over his sexual desires and activities. Like thousands of his contemporaries, Wittgenstein had become convinced that the sort of high spiritual and intellectual creativity that he craved was virtually incompatible with sexual activity. It is often remarked that Wittgenstein admired the work of Otto

[8] Bertrand Russell, *Autobiography* (London: George Allen and Unwin, 1968), Vol. II, p. 136. Leonard Woolf contests Russell's description in the final volume of his own memoirs, speaking of Wittgenstein's aggressively cruel streak. See Leonard Woolf, *The Journey Not the Arrival Matters* (London: The Hogarth Press, 1969), p. 48.

[4] Paul Engelmann, *Letters from Ludwig Wittgenstein with a Memoir* (Oxford: Basil Blackwell, 1967), p. 57.

Weininger, but rarely explained that Weininger's fame stemmed from his extraordinary misogyny, his sustained and impassioned argument that women are inevitably inferior to men. Although Weininger rather reluctantly concedes that women are human, he argues vehemently that they lack souls and are incapable of genius. Worse, physical contact with women despiritualizes men. Thus Weininger advocated absolute sexual abstinence as a precondition of spiritual development and genius. Those today who tend to dismiss Weininger as a crank must remember, if they are to understand the subterranean currents of Central European thought before and after the First World War, that many of Weininger's contemporaries took him dead seriously: between 1903 and 1923 *Geschlecht und Charakter (Sex and Character)* went through twenty-five editions, and by 1923 the book had been translated into some eight tongues. Sigmund Freud, who had read Weininger's book in manuscript,[5] incorporated similar views about the clash between sexual activity and high spirituality in his own theory of sublimation, and is said to have abandoned sexual activity for this reason—as also did Gandhi.[6] Wittgenstein's English contemporary, J. D. Unwin, pushed such an outlook a step further in his own best-selling book *Sex and Culture*, in which, after examining some eighty societies,

[5] Vincent Brome, *Freud and His Early Circle* (New York: William Morrow and Company, Inc., 1968), p. 9.

[6] See Sigmund Freud, *Civilization and Its Discontents*, or *Two Short Accounts of Psycho-Analysis* (Penguin Books, 1962), and many passages in Freud's writings. See also Ernest Jones, *The Life and Work of Sigmund Freud* (New York: Basic Books, 1953–57); and Erik H. Erikson, *Gandhi's Truth* (New York: W. W. Norton and Company, Inc., 1969).

he came to the conclusion—one that he claimed harmonized with Freudian teaching—that anthropological evidence established sexual promiscuity and cultural achievement to be inversely proportional. Yet another of Wittgenstein's heroes, Leo Tolstoy, eventually, though reluctantly, also came to advocate celibacy.[7]

I have mentioned only comparatively well-known names, and names of thinkers who—with the possible exception of Gandhi—influenced Wittgenstein.[8] Another quite obscure writer also needs mentioning here, for possibly he had the profoundest effect of all: Dr. Ludwig Hänsel, with whom Wittgenstein struck up a friendship during their internment at Monte Cassino. An Austrian like himself, Hänsel was then already a schoolteacher by profession, and later became professor at a Gymnasium in Vienna. A puritanical Roman Catholic of talents far inferior to those of Wittgenstein, Hänsel nonetheless played a role akin to spiritual adviser and father confessor to Wittgenstein throughout his life. Although Hänsel had some philosophical pretensions (Wittgenstein had met him at a course in logic which Hänsel was conducting in the POW camp), his primary concern was with education, and his preoccupation there was with the sexual purity of boys. Some years later he published *Die Jugend und die leibliche Liebe* (*Youth*

[7] Leo Tolstoy, "What I Believe," in Volume II of *The Works of Leo Tolstoy* (London: Oxford University Press, 1933), pp. 526–27; but more especially in his *Kreutzer Sonata* and in the *Afterword* thereto.

[8] As is well known, Wittgenstein was especially fond of the work of the Indian poet Rabindranath Tagore. Thus it is by no means impossible that Wittgenstein also knew of Gandhi's teaching. Tagore did know and write about Gandhi, and Gandhi too had been much inspired by Tolstoy.

*and Carnal Love*), a polemical tract against masturbation (contrary to nature and damaging to body and soul), against homosexuality, and against Freud, who "unfortunately had no understanding of morals and religion." [9] Evidently, although he had no illusions about Hänsel's talents, Wittgenstein came to rely on him for an odd sort of moral support. His encounter with Hänsel also played a significant role in leading Wittgenstein himself to become a schoolteacher on his release from the prisoner-of-war camp.

## II

What Wittgenstein called his "second dream" came to him some two years later, possibly in early December 1920, in Trattenbach. A rather more complicated dream, it goes as follows:

I was a priest. In the front hall of my house there was an altar; to the right of the altar a stairway led off. It was a grand stairway carpeted in red, rather like that at the Alleegasse.[10] At the foot of the altar, and partly covering it, was an oriental carpet. And certain other religious objects and regalia were placed on and beside the altar. One of these was a rod of precious metal.

[9] Ludwig Hänsel, *Die Jugend und die leibliche Liebe: Sexualpädagogische Betrachtungen* (Innsbruck-Vienna-Munich: Tyrolia Verlag, 1938), bearing the imprimatur of the Viennese archdiocese of 8 January 1938.

[10] The reference is to the Palais Wittgenstein, home of Wittgenstein's parents and family, purchased in 1890 by his father. It was located on Alleegasse, a street that was later renamed the Argentinierstraße. Seriously bombed during the Second World War, the building has since been demolished.

But a theft occurred. A thief entered from the left and stole the rod. This had to be reported to the police, who sent a representative who wanted a description of the rod. For instance, of what sort of metal was it made? I could not say; I could not even say whether it was of silver or of gold. The police officer questioned whether the rod had ever existed in the first place. I then began to examine the other parts and fittings of the altar and noticed that the carpet was a prayer rug. My eyes began to focus on the border of the rug. The border was lighter in colour than the beautiful center. In a curious way it seemed to be faded. It was, nonetheless, still strong and firm.

Wittgenstein was never confident about how to interpret this dream, but he regarded it as most important: it is one source of his conviction that he had been "called," [11] and of his recurring notion that he ought perhaps to become a monk. Shortly after experiencing this dream he acquired a bamboo walking stick, which he carried constantly for many years.

Both of Wittgenstein's dreams are beautiful; both are deeply religious; the focus in both dreams—in the first dream at the beginning, in the second dream at the end—comes to rest on the prayer rug, with its contained and spiritualized phallus. In the second dream Wittgenstein himself is serving at the sacrificial altar, which occupies a central place between the stairs at the right and an undefined *sinister* place at the left, wherein and wherefrom such things as thefts can originate. Witt-

[11] See Ludwig Hänsel, "Ludwig Wittgenstein (1889–1951)," in *Wissenschaft und Weltbild, Monatschrift für alle Gebiete der Forschung*, Vol. VIII, October 4, 1951, pp. 315–23, especially p. 322. "One night, during the time when he was a teacher, he had the feeling that he had been called but had refused."

genstein, who by the time he had this dream had read a lot of Freud, made the association just mentioned between right and left, and identified the stairs as symbols indicating an upward path toward spiritual growth. The rod seemed at once obvious and bewildering. It was in an obvious sense a phallic object, and one rich in associations with serpents. For example, in Exodus (Chapters 4 and 7) the rods of Moses and Aaron, when cast on the ground, become serpents; and Aaron's rod devours the serpent-rods of the Egyptian magicians. A double reference to Aaron's rod is possible here: in the seventeenth chapter of the Biblical book of Numbers, Aaron, the first high priest of the Israelites, and his descendants in perpetuity are set apart from the rest of Israel for the priesthood following an incident when Aaron's rod, placed beside rods representing each of the tribes of Israel, quickly buds, blossoms, and bears almonds. Aaron's rod then became one of the most sacred religious objects of the wandering Israelites and was placed in the Ark of the Covenant along with the pot of manna and the tables of the Law. Wittgenstein discussed the connections I have just mentioned, but they appear to have come to him as suggestions for interpretation from some other party, possibly from Hänsel, who, unlike Wittgenstein, was well acquainted with the Old Testament. It puzzled Wittgenstein to think that *if* such an interpretation were to be attached to the dream, it would be *his* dream. An object made of precious metal more likely to be stolen would, at least in the Christian ritual, be the grail or chalice, long associated in myth and legend with the female. Possibly Wittgenstein's homosexuality would account for the absence from his dream's altar of the chalice and the substitution of a more archaic, more masculine symbol of the rod. Wittgenstein found this idea a speculative dead end.

An interpretation which struck him as more likely, and which occurred to him spontaneously, was to regard the rod as both a phallic symbol and a *pestle*, as in the mortar and pestle of chemists and alchemists. For some sort of transformation, including a possible transmutation of substance, seems to be indicated in the dream. At first, attention is focused on the rod of precious metal; it disappears, the preciousness of its metal is doubted—in effect, precious metal is transformed into base metal; and then the rod's very existence is questioned. Only then is attention transferred to the prayer rug, wherein the rod reappears in spiritualized form.

As for the thief and the policeman, two other figures in the dream, Wittgenstein made associations of a fairly routine sort. The theft of the rod from the altar he associated with the Promethean theft of fire from the gods; the police, with the voice of conscience or parental authority. But he was never able to weave the various components of the dream into a coherent whole. And it would be foolhardy to make any such attempt some fifty years after the dream occurred, and more than twenty years after Wittgenstein's death.

What does strike one is the connection between this dream and the first dream. The prayer rug recurs. But in the second dream the rod-serpent, which had been so active and forbidding in the first dream, is snatched away, and it is even suggested that it is illusory, a kind of *maya*. The prayer rug, on the other hand, no longer furnishes a room but rather adorns an altar of sacrifice,

and it may be closely examined by the tortured philos-
opher-priest who serves at that altar. Yet the prayer rug
is strangely unnoticed by this priest until *after* the
disappearance of the phallic rod. It was as if the integrated spiritualized phallus became accessible to him
only after the disappearance—the theft or even self-
castration—of the rod.

The dream is fascinating, and could be examined
at great length. What is important here is that Wittgenstein regarded it as a "good dream," pointing toward
a resolution of his fundamental conflict, and that it
came at a time when he was working out a self-protective
pattern of behavior to shield him from his most extreme
tendencies toward promiscuously homosexual behavior.
Such action seemed to him to be urgently necessary, for
the conflict which is so vividly portrayed in the first
dream had come to a head in his life during the year
preceding the second dream. Indeed, it virtually exploded
within him in October 1919 and again in April 1920.


## III


That October of 1919 had proved to be one of the cruelest months that Wittgenstein was to endure, cruel not
only because of his intense hatred of the actions he performed during its passing weeks, but also because the
pattern of behavior fixed during this interlude was to
return repeatedly to torture him. It would have been
hard for him in the best of times, but he was, in fact,
at his lowest ebb physically and psychologically.

Wittgenstein had reached Neuwaldegg, the family

summer home in Vienna, from Monte Cassino on Monday, August 25, 1919. The following day his military discharge was made official. It had been little more than a year that Wittgenstein had spent away from Vienna; early the preceding August, on military leave at Neuwaldegg, he had brought to completion the book which later came to be called the *Tractatus Logico-Philosophicus* and had submitted it to the publishers Jahoda and Siegel. In the few months following Wittgenstein's departure from Vienna for the very last phase of the war, his and his family's situation had been transformed. On 13 August, 1918, Wittgenstein's favorite uncle, Paul Wittgenstein, whom, together with Bertrand Russell, he had thanked in the preface to his newly completed manuscript, had died. By the 25th of October, 1918, Wittgenstein knew that Jahoda had rejected his manuscript; two days later Ludwig's brother Kurt shot himself when the troops under his command abandoned the field. On 3 November Wittgenstein himself had been taken prisoner at Trent by Italian troops. The Austro-Hungarian Monarchy had tottered and fallen and had been dismembered; the Revolution had occurred; news reached Wittgenstein that his Cambridge friend David Pinsent, whom he had loved deeply, had been killed in action the preceding May. After nine months in prison, a physically and mentally debilitated Ludwig Wittgenstein returned to Vienna to find himself the only son of Karl Wittgenstein who remained reasonably intact. He was greeted by his mother, widowed in January 1913; his eldest and favorite sister, Hermine, known as Mining; his sister Margarete Stonborough, whom he both loved and fought all his life; his sister Helene

Salzer, whom he disliked; and his brother Paul, hailed at his debut in 1913 as one of the most promising pianists in Europe. Paul had lost his right arm on the Russian front early in the war and had been returned to Vienna where, with remarkable energy, he learned to play the piano prodigiously well with his left hand alone. Ironically, all that were really intact in the family were the estates and the fortune; indeed, Wittgenstein returned to Vienna one of the richest men in Europe.

Before his death on 20 January 1913, Karl Wittgenstein, founder of the Austrian iron and steel industry, had transferred virtually all his liquid capital to American stocks and bonds, principally in the United States Steel Corporation. And thus the fortune, which was giving Ludwig alone an annual income of 300,000 kronen (gold crowns) in 1914, prior to the start of the war,[12] had been vastly augmented by the prosperity of the forces which had helped bring about his own country's defeat. As for the money that had been left in Austria during the war, for the most part Karl Wittgenstein's brother Ludwig, who had managed it, invested it in government bonds. But prior to the end of the war and the great inflation, he had sold most of the war bonds to buy real estate, one of the few things in Austria whose value was augmented by the inflation. Nor was the fortune to be dissipated in the years that followed: what was needed

[12] Known from army records. According to Austrian National Bank authorities in Vienna, 300,000 kronen (1914) would be equivalent in buying power for 1969 to 4,587,000 Austrian schillings, or approximately $185,000.00. If so, the capital on which the income was based could easily have been the 1969 equivalent of two million U.S. dollars. This would depend, of course, on how the income-producing money was invested.

for the operating costs of the family was returned as required to Austria. But the bulk of the fortune was, for most of the interwar period, invested in Holland, relatively safe from the inflation that wiped out many rich families of Germany and Austria.

It takes little imagination to perceive how such a contradictory situation would have affected a man of the sensitivity of Ludwig Wittgenstein. Although his brother Paul and he would eventually become more famous than their father, there was little at that moment to suggest that they were other than a cripple and an exhausted veteran, the latter on the brink of suicide. Ludwig now talked of suicide incessantly, thereby—and with good reason—terrifying his sisters Mining and Margarete.

Kurt, it has been noted, took his life at the very end of the war. He was the third Wittgenstein brother to commit suicide. The eldest brother, Hans, a musical genius who had begun composing when four years old, had taken his life in Havana, Cuba, in April 1902, in his twenty-fourth year. The third son, Rudolf, killed himself in Vienna on May 2, 1904. Hans was known by the family to have been homosexual; Rudolf is thought to have been so.

In addition to these suicides within his immediate family, another suicide, apart from Weininger's, had affected Ludwig deeply: Ludwig Bolzmann, the great Austrian physicist with whom the adolescent Ludwig Wittgenstein had aspired to study, committed suicide in 1906, the year of Wittgenstein's graduation from secondary school.

In such a context there is no reason to suppose that Wittgenstein was less than serious in his own talk of suicide. He had, in fact, been thinking and talking of suicide for years under far less trying circumstances than those he faced in 1919. In 1912, when he was twenty-three, Ludwig confessed to David Pinsent that he had suffered from a terrible loneliness for some nine years, with thoughts of suicide constantly in his mind. That nine-year period to which Wittgenstein referred must have begun somewhere between 1902 and 1904, a time of enormous crisis and strain for all the members of his family, and perhaps especially for Ludwig, who, at fourteen years of age, may be presumed to have been undergoing the usual crises of puberty. In 1913 Wittgenstein had alarmed Bertrand Russell with talk of suicide. In 1920 Wittgenstein told his schoolteacher colleague Martin Scherleitner, in Trattenbach, that he had originally volunteered to serve in the First World War in order to find death, as a method of suicide; and the theme of suicide recurs repeatedly in Wittgenstein's wartime and postwar correspondence with his friend Paul Engelmann.

In these circumstances, Wittgenstein made two decisions on his arrival in Vienna. The first, which he had already formed during his internment, and which had been urged on him by Hänsel, was to prepare for a career as an elementary schoolteacher. Margarete and Mining welcomed this as work therapy for their brother, and it was probably Margarete who informed Wittgenstein on his return of the new possibilities available in schoolteaching through the "School Reform Movement," to be discussed below, and who made arrangements for him through her friend Otto Glöckel, leader and administrative head of Austrian school reform. At any rate, Wittgenstein reported his decision to Engelmann on the second of September, just one week after his discharge from the army, and by September 16 he was enrolled in the Lehrerbildungsanstalt in the Kundmanngasse, one of the first Teacher Training Colleges operating under Glöckel's general direction.

Wittgenstein's second step was to divest himself of his fortune. The idea was his own and was insisted upon with almost insane passion. A member of his family reports that he caused enormous commotion by appearing suddenly at his bankers' one morning to declare that he wanted nothing more to do with his money and that it must be disposed of forthwith. In the event, his entire liquid fortune was given to his brother and sisters. Rather elaborate steps had to be taken formally to distribute the money as Wittgenstein wished, with special measures being taken to ensure that none of the money at that time under temporary sequestration in America should ever come into Wittgenstein's hands. Despite the commotion there was no thought of charity in the transfer, and the decision seems to have been carefully reviewed by the family. Ludwig Wittgenstein was considered by his brother and sisters, and in particular by his Uncle Ludwig, to be in no condition to look after his inheritance in any case; there was the threat of suicide, with the possibility of further complications connected with death duty attached to a widely dispersed and partly sequestered fortune. So Uncle Ludwig approved the transfer to Mining, Margarete and Paul, with the understanding that they should in effect hold it in trust for him in case he should ever want it back. This they did faithfully until the middle and late thirties when—with the approach of war and the possibility that the money would be confiscated by the Nazis in case Wittgenstein's siblings were ruled to be Jews under the Nuremberg laws—the money was distributed among Wittgenstein's nephews and nieces.

These steps having been taken, Wittgenstein moved from the shelter of his family at Neuwaldegg on the outskirts of Vienna, and, also refusing to live at the Palais Wittgenstein, the town mansion near the center city, took up lodgings nearby, in rooms on Untere Viaduktgasse in Vienna's third district. These quarters, only ten minutes' walk from the Palais Wittgenstein on the Alleegasse, were apparently selected by Wittgenstein in large measure for their convenience to both home and school. Untere Viaduktgasse was close not only to the family palace on the edge of the fourth district but also to his sister Margarete's flat on the Rennweg; and it was only six streets to the north of the Kundmanngasse, where stood the Teachers Training College which he was now attending, and where he was later to build a great house for his sister. By September 25, 1919, he was settled in Untere Viaduktgasse, and the month of October, described at the beginning of this section as his cruelest month, was about to begin—although, in retrospect, it is just possible that the source of his suffering during October was also what prevented him from taking his life.


## IV


Wittgenstein was now to find the third district, selected for its convenience, convenient in an unexpected way.

By walking for ten minutes to the east, down Marxer-gasse and over the Sophienbrücke (now called the Rotundenbrücke), he could quickly reach the parkland meadows of the Prater, where rough young men were ready to cater to him sexually. Once he had discovered this place, Wittgenstein found to his horror that he could scarcely keep away from it. Several nights each week he would break away from his rooms and make the quick walk to the Prater, possessed, as he put it to friends, by a demon he could barely control. Wittgenstein found he much preferred the sort of rough blunt homosexual youth that he could find strolling in the paths and alleys of the Prater to those ostensibly more refined young men who frequented the Sirk Ecke in the Kärtnerstraße and the neighboring bars at the edge of the inner city. And it was to this particular spot—still used for the same pur-pose at night, and still about as dangerous—that Witt-genstein was to hie almost as long as he lived in or visited Vienna. Similarly, in later years in England he was from time to time to flee the fashionable and intellectual young men who were ready to place themselves at his dis-posal in Cambridge, in favor of the company of tough boys in London pubs.

Happily, Wittgenstein came to meet a hetero-sexual young automobile mechanic, Arvid Sjögren, who was later to marry into the Wittgenstein family. By November Wittgenstein had moved far from the third dis-trict into the large and pleasant home of Sjögren and his family in Hietzing, from which he had to ride the Stadt-bahn to attend school and visit his family. By living closely and intimately with the Sjögrens, Wittgenstein began to experience a way of protecting himself from himself. But in April 1920 he was forced to break off his association with Sjögren temporarily, and literally to flee from the Sjögren household: Sjögren's mother had fallen in love with him! The story has the makings of a comic opera; but for Wittgenstein personally it was a tragic accident, for he returned, almost inevitably, to rooms in the third district, this time in the Rasumofskygasse, even closer to the Sophienbrücke and to the Prater. It was during this period that he engaged in perhaps the most promiscuous behavior of his life. On the last day of this month, referring to his way of life, he wrote to his friend Paul Engelmann in Olmütz: "Things have gone utterly miserably for me lately. Of course only because of my own baseness and rottenness. I have continually thought about taking my own life, and now too this thought still haunts me. *I have sunk to the bottom.* May you never be in that position!" [13]

## V

When one is terrified, as was Wittgenstein, of what one might do, one may attempt to construct an environment that will help to protect one from doing what one in a sense wants but must not do. This Wittgenstein did; and in the pattern of his construction is to be found some explanation for some of his odder actions.

Wittgenstein would seek milieux or situations satisfying two conditions: to be removed from the temptation of easy and casual sexual relationships with street youths, and such like; and to be surrounded by youths with

[13] Engelmann, *op. cit.*, p. 32.

On the Hochreit, summer 1920. Wittgenstein is seated between his sister Helene Salzer and his friend, Arvid Sjögren.

whom he could enjoy platonic relationships that would "bring him to life." Thus a series of close friendships developed with good-looking young men of sweet and docile disposition, some insight but no "cleverness," toward whom Wittgenstein could become emotionally very much attached. Such young men have been characterized as the "type" for whom Wittgenstein "fell" repeatedly, from his youth to the final decade of his life. It was in this way and in part to play this role that many young men, including some of his favored Cambridge friends and students, entered his life. All were physically attractive, "with nice faces," as Wittgenstein put it. All of them he could dominate easily, and he could relax in their company. And their companionship would distract and protect him from the loneliness that would send him stalking into the night in search of sex. The other strategy that Wittgenstein used to protect himself from himself was simply to avoid "danger areas," such as Vienna, Manchester and London, where casual and impersonal sex without any intellectual or spiritual dimension was easily come by: thus his monklike retreats to Norway, to the isolated villages of Semmering in lower Austria, and even to Cambridge.

Ludwig Wittgenstein's friendships, then, he used as moral encounters; within them he became creative, intimate, even playful. Sex was immoral; by and large it was not for friends.

And so Wittgenstein was to live. His life was lived in a kind of mourning, as it were, that he could not escape from sex entirely. For there recurred throughout his life episodes which he regarded as relapses, during which he would plunge into fleeting relationships with anonymous youths encountered in the dark and never met again. The second dream, the dream which he regarded as a token of his "call," haunted him after such episodes, and he condemned himself ruthlessly for his adventures. About a year after his second dream, on the second of January 1921, Wittgenstein wrote again to Engelmann:

I have been morally dead for more than a year. . . . I am one of those cases which perhaps are not all that rare today: I had a task, did not do it, and now the failure is wrecking my life. I ought to have done something positive with my life, to have become a star in the sky. Instead of which I remained stuck on earth, and now I am gradually fading out. My life has really become meaningless and so it consists only of futile episodes. The people around me do not notice this and would not understand; but I know that I have a fundamental deficiency. Be glad of it, if you don't understand what I am writing here.

As one reads this wistful, sad and moving letter, one can almost see Wittgenstein gazing in through that forbidding window or standing before his altar, his eyes trained on the prayer-rug treasure that he was never quite to obtain. Yet we know today that what he wrote in his letter was hardly correct. Far from gradually fading out, his star was to soar during the next fifty years, and to transform philosophical activity. It is sometimes said that Wittgenstein lived his life on the edge of madness. It is just possible that those "futile episodes" which he occasionally permitted himself provided the sort of release that helped keep him sane and alive. Weininger, after all, did commit suicide.

# 2

## THE PROPOSITION

🔃 🔃 🔃

### I

During these years immediately following the war, the manuscript of Wittgenstein's *Tractatus Logico-Philosophicus* was being shuttled forlornly from publisher to publisher. The details of the many rejections, and the numerous misunderstandings and delays which kept it from being published in book form until 1922, have been carefully chronicled by Georg Henrik von Wright.[1] Wittgenstein had titled the manuscript "Der Satz," or "The Proposition," and it was not until shortly before publication that the book acquired the Latin title suggested by G. E. Moore.[2]

If one is to have any hope of seeing what connection the *Tractatus* might have with Wittgenstein's life, the first question to ask about it is this: Why was this book about propositions—statements of scientific fact—written in the first place, and what problem or set of problems was it meant to solve? Although it is easy to list answers to this question, few survive examination.

Some sections of the book, of a rather technical char-

[1] Georg Henrik von Wright, "Die Entstehung des Tractatus Logico-Philosophicus," in Ludwig Wittgenstein, *Briefe an Ludwig von Ficker* (Salzburg: Otto Müller Verlag, 1969), pp. 71–110.

[2] I received this information from some of Wittgenstein's former colleagues in Semmering, who saw his copy of the manuscript during his stint as a village schoolteacher.

acter, are obviously, and usually explicitly, meant to further, and in some cases to correct, the work of Gottlob Frege and Bertrand Russell in the foundations of mathematics and logic. Interesting and important as these sections of the book may be, the book was not composed merely to answer such questions. We are concerned here with the main thrust of the book, not with its details.

Anthony Quinton has suggested [3] that the *Tractatus* sets out to answer a Kantian-style question, to wit: "How is language possible?" Yet not every question of the form: "How is *x* possible?" is Kantian in character. For a question of this sort to be Kantian, it would have to be set in the context of some theory or presupposition which made the existence of language seem impossible— or at least doubtful. Kant raised his question about the possibility of synthetic a priori knowledge, for instance, in the face of (1) the patent existence of knowledge of this sort (which for Kant included mathematics and part of Newtonian physics) and (2) a Humean theory of knowledge in terms of which such knowledge was impossible. According to a theory of knowledge then widely prevailing, such knowledge was impossible; yet it existed. And thus the question.

No such question about language is present in Wittgenstein's *Tractatus*. One of the things he wants to determine is what conditions must obtain if a precisely mean-

[3] Anthony Quinton, "Contemporary British Philosophy," in A *Critical History of Western Philosophy*, ed. D. J. O'Connor (Glencoe: The Free Press, 1964), p. 536. The same suggestion is made by Peter Hacker in "Nets of Language," *Encounter*, April 1971, p. 85; and a similar suggestion appears in Stephen Toulmin, "Ludwig Wittgenstein," *Encounter*, January 1969.

ingful language is to exist. But the presumption in the early writing is that these conditions do exist; the Kantian dilemma does not arise. To see a truly Kantian-style question about the possibility of language, one might by contrast turn to Noam Chomsky, who argues in *Language and Mind* (1968) that the learning theories of behavioristic psychology and empiricist philosophy, to which many contemporary linguists adhere, simply cannot account for the acquisition or learning of grammar and language. If empiricist assumptions about language acquisition are correct, then language is impossible. Chomsky sets out to escape this Kantian-style dilemma, just as Kant himself did, through a critique of contemporary empiricism. The question as to what extent other Kantian themes may be present in the *Tractatus* will be considered below. Meanwhile, it is clear that Wittgenstein was not, whatever he was doing, concerned with the question attributed to him by Quinton.

## II

Another common answer about the nature of Wittgenstein's *Tractatus* is that he was attempting, like Kant, to draw a line of demarcation between science and nonscience. As far as it goes, the answer is correct: this line of demarcation corresponds to that between factual and nonfactual language. But the question then arises: why did Wittgenstein want to do that? It is easy to explain why some philosophers have wanted to draw such a line, but harder to state what Wittgenstein's precise intention was. Most often, the demarcation between science and nonscience has been drawn for the purpose of evaluation and criticism. It has been assumed by many philosophers —perhaps most conspicuously in this century by the logical positivists of the Vienna School—that the way to demarcate good theories from bad theories, legitimate ideas from illegitimate ones, was to demarcate the scientific from the nonscientific. One could even write an acceptance and rejection rule in terms of the demarcation, to wit: "When in doubt about the merits of some particular idea, theory, proposal, or whatever, first determine if it is scientific. If it is, classify it as legitimate; if it is not, reject it."

More than a suggestion of such an approach appears in the *Tractatus*: indeed, it is sufficiently strong to have led many interpreters of his thought to suppose that Wittgenstein's basic aim was to *condemn* as meaningless whatever could not be classified according to his criteria as factual or scientific. Yet other tendencies in the *Tractatus* prevent one from accepting this as its author's intention.

On the one hand, Wittgenstein himself states his aim as "to set a limit . . . to the expression of thoughts." He writes: "The whole sense of the book might be summed up in the following words: what can be said at all can be said clearly, and what we cannot talk about we must pass over in silence." As he put it: "The correct method in philosophy would really be the following: to say nothing except what can be said, i.e., propositions of natural science,—i.e., something that has nothing to do with philosophy—and then, whenever someone else wanted to say something metaphysical, to demonstrate to him that he had failed to give a meaning to certain signs in his propositions." (6.53)

Not only is pre-Kantian speculative metaphysics excluded from the "sayable" and meaningful by Wittgenstein's criteria—a more detailed account of which will be sketched below—so are universal laws of nature, the "elucidatory" statements of the *Tractatus* itself, logic, ethics and aesthetics, philosophy, religion. Yet at most only speculative metaphysics is condemned outright. Logic, ethics and aesthetics, and religion, while described as "transcendental," are not condemned. And the philosophical statements of the *Tractatus* are taken to be elucidative in a most helpful way, despite their "meaninglessness."

While declaring that ethics is meaningless, Wittgenstein nonetheless reported to his friends Ludwig von Ficker and Paul Engelmann that the whole point of the book was ethical. As Wittgenstein explained to von Ficker,

The book's point is an ethical one. I once meant to include in the preface a sentence which is not in fact there now but which I will write out for you here, because it will perhaps be a key to the work for you. What I meant to write, then, was this: My work consists of two parts: the one presented here plus all that I have *not* written. And it is precisely this second part that is the important one. My book draws limits to the sphere of the ethical from the inside as it were, and I am convinced that this is the ONLY *rigorous* way of drawing those limits. In short, I believe that where *many* others today are just *gassing*, I have managed in my book to put everything firmly into place by being silent about it. And for that reason, unless I am very much mis-

taken, the book will say a great deal that you yourself want
to say. Only perhaps you won't see that it is said in the
book. For now, I would recommend you to read the *preface*
and the *conclusion*, because they contain the most direct
expression of the point of the book.[4]

### III

It is, then, only in a rather odd sense of the word that
the demarcation between science and nonscience, as it
appears in the *Tractatus*, is a matter of evaluation. Nonscience is not *condemned*, but it is suggested that it is in
bad taste—indeed, virtually immoral—even to *try* to talk
about it. For that leads inevitably to gassing. The evaluation here, such as it is, is of an ascetic, aristocratic,
elitist character. It is implied that those few who *can*
understand Wittgenstein would know better than to—
would have better taste than to—indulge in metaphysics
or in moralizing, or, for that matter, in *anti*metaphysics.
Wittgenstein does not suppose that his views will win
wide support as, say, a useful measure for sorting out
nonsense. Quite the contrary, in his Preface and in several letters he expressed doubt that anyone, even Russell
and Frege, would understand him, let alone be capable of
practicing his demarcation.

Just as fastidiously as he himself advocates silence
Wittgenstein avoids imposing his own silence on others.
*Noblesse oblige:* a personal elitism is accompanied by a
radical tolerance for those who either did not or could not
live by a similar code. These were not to be condemned;

[4] Ludwig Wittgenstein, *Briefe an Ludwig von Ficker* (Salzburg: Otto Müller Verlag, 1969), pp. 35-36. Quoted in
English translation in Paul Engelmann, *op. cit.*, pp. 143-44.

they were parts of forms of life in which one did not participate and about which one did not speak. There are, of course, dangers here: some silence is deep and some stems from having little or nothing to say. Wittgenstein provides no criterion to distinguish one kind of silence from the other.

Here the contrast between Wittgenstein and the members of the Vienna Circle with whom his ideas later became associated is particularly striking. For several prominent members of the Circle tended to think of it as a kind of embryonic political party embracing an ideology with potential mass appeal. Otto Neurath, in particular, who has been described as the "party secretary" of the Circle, certainly had ambitious political aims for the widespread dissemination of the ideology of logical positivism. Indeed, he went so far as to encourage the members of the group to drop the name "positivism" in favor of "physicalism." "Positivism" was objectionable to Marxists on several counts: for one thing, Lenin had denounced an earlier version of positivism as bourgeois; for another, Friedrich Adler, one of the most eminent theoreticians of the Austrian Social Democratic Party, had used Ernst Mach's version of positivism to support his critique of Marx's materialism. Neurath, however, who had been a member of the short-lived Spartacist Communist government in Munich at the end of the First World War, imagined that he could persuade Stalin to adopt a philosophy called "physicalism"—a word with connotations close to "materialism"—as the official doctrine of the Soviet Union. Neurath naïvely traveled to the Soviet Union on behalf of this cause, but he was not successful.

On the other hand, one *can* find attitudes toward
language reminiscent of Wittgenstein's among his contemporary Viennese, but not so much among the philosophers as among the Austrian writers and litterateurs.

## IV

Perhaps the most appropriate example is that of Hugo
von Hofmannsthal, one of several turn-of-the-century
Austrian writers who voiced their loss of confidence in
the power of speech. Hofmannsthal is often bracketed
with Karl Kraus, Franz Kafka, and Fritz Mauthner; and
in his way, he shared with them the worry that speech
was becoming a vehicle not of communication but of
mendacity and pointlessness. Kafka had written, in
rather obvious parables, of royal messengers who rush
through the world with proclamations that no longer
possess meaning. With tremendous energy Karl Kraus
turned out his periodical *Die Fackel* almost single-
handedly, scornfully attacking almost all of the other
periodicals and newspapers of the land for their distortion of language and parading examples of their literary
errors. Mauthner came to wonder whether language
could survive as a means of responsible communication.
Nonetheless, apart from their common conviction, surely
correct, that language is subject to abuse and misuse,
these writers are very dissimilar. Wittgenstein knew
Kraus's work and admired his early publications; he was
also acquainted with Mauthner's work and even quoted

him in the *Tractatus,* although in disagreement. But their ideas are far apart.[5]

With Hofmannsthal, however, Wittgenstein did have more in common. From his first verse play, *Yesterday* (1891), to his classic comedy *The Difficult Man* (1921), Hofmannsthal elaborated on the themes of his famous *Letter to Lord Chandos:* not simply the inadequacy, but the *disgusting indecency* of talk—particularly talk about morality, about politics, about literature and aesthetics. Already in 1895, in reviewing a book on the actor Friedrich Mitterwurzer, Hofmannsthal wrote:

People are tired of listening to talk. They feel a deep disgust with words. For words have pushed themselves in front of things. . . . We are in the grip of a horrible process in which thought is utterly stifled by concepts. Hardly anyone now is capable of being sure in his own mind about what he understands, what he does not understand, of saying what he feels and what he does not feel. This has awakened a desperate love for all those arts which are executed without speech. . . .[6]

Such aesthetic and ethical insistence on the indecent gassing of most speech recurs throughout Hofmannsthal's work, being most vividly expressed by the "Difficult Man" himself, the Count Hans Karl Bühl, who, when asked after his return from the war to deliver a speech in the Austrian House of Lords, demands: "Am I supposed to stand up and make a speech about peace among peo-

[5] Compare Gershon Weiler, *Mauthner's Critique of Language* (Cambridge: Cambridge University Press, 1970). The *later* ideas of Wittgenstein do bear some similarity to those of Mauthner.

[6] Hugo von Hofmannsthal, *Selected Plays and Libretti,* ed. Michael Hamburger (New York: Pantheon Books, 1963), p. xvii.

ples and the unitedness of nations—I, a man whose sole conviction is that it's impossible to open one's mouth without causing the most ineradicable confusion? . . . Am I to let loose a flood of words every one of which will seem positively indecent to me?" [7]

Hofmannsthal and Wittgenstein were different personalities indeed, and it would be folly to exaggerate their similarities, even in their aesthetic preferences, let alone their philosophical views. But the fastidious reverence in which both Wittgenstein and Hofmannsthal held language—it is no accident that Hans Karl Bühl is a Count—helps illuminate Wittgenstein's oblique, indirect, evasive behavior toward the members of the Vienna Circle. Like Hofmannsthal's "Difficult Man," Wittgenstein was pursued and pressured by these more public men to join the philosophical arena, to attend their meetings, to proclaim his philosophy. He responded with *distance*, by evading philosophical discussion, by reading from Tagore and other poets to the members of the Circle who came to meetings and coffee houses expecting to hear him explain the *Tractatus*. Occasionally he would be delightfully exasperating and just whistle to them from his extraordinary repertoire of classical music. With some members of the Circle—in particular Carnap and Neurath, whose antimetaphysical positivism struck him as vulgarian—Wittgenstein went to precautions more elaborate than those of the Count in *The Difficult Man* in order to avoid encounters. It was only with such people as Schlick and Waismann, "because of their high culture and refined tastes," that he would eventually discuss philosophy in the late twenties. As Engelmann reports

[7] *Ibid.*, p. 820.

(page 118): "Wittgenstein found Schlick a distinguished and understanding partner in discussion, all the more so because he appreciated Schlick's highly cultured personality—something which Wittgenstein always found essential in his intellectual contacts with others."

## V

The question may well be raised to what extent were the worries Wittgenstein and Hofmannsthal expressed about the capacity of language—in particular the language of morals, aesthetics, religion, and the emotions—well founded? To what extent were they, rather, an exaggerated response to a period of sloppy and overgrown misuse of language that accompanied the cataclysmic social changes of the German-speaking world during the latter part of the nineteenth century and the early part of this century?

No doubt the German language was undergoing a period of considerable change at this time. All languages and modes of communication, however, experience periods of change—sometimes of expansion, sometimes of compression. Wittgenstein and Hofmannsthal appear to have wanted compression and restraint. There is nothing new about that: in some of the most creative periods of Chinese painting, to take an example from another mode of expression, the crucial part of a picture was what had been left out. And one picture, of course, "is worth a thousand words."

Poetry too is often likened to a process of compression, of conveying a great deal through leaving much more unsaid. Ezra Pound and Arthur Koestler, among others, have claimed that *Dichtung,* the German word for poetry, is related etymologically to *dichten,* which means "to compress." The etymology happens to be incorrect, but the idea behind it reflects a common assumption about language.

Nor was language the only mode of expression undergoing significant change during this time. Painters, architects and musicians were also, at the beginning of the century, radically reexamining their media. Influenced by the French, painters turned from representational painting to a variety of new modes of expression. Among architects, the Bauhaus school in Germany and the work of Adolf Loos in Vienna, with its studied avoidance of ornamentation, had an important influence on Wittgenstein. Musicians, notably in Vienna, abandoned the diatonic system of scales and modulations: Arnold Schönberg is a conspicuous example.

Some historians and literary critics [8] have piled example on example to convey more an image than a thesis about this period, an image suggesting that the German language was, at the turn of the century, on the verge of collapse; that the various critiques of language produced then—whether by Mauthner, Wittgenstein, Kraus, or Hofmannsthal—were all responding, in a rather parallel way, to this crisis; and that, moreover, the route out of it lay more or less in the direction in which Wittgenstein and Hofmannsthal had pointed—in a recognition of some sort of "significant silence."

That those who have made such diagnoses and sug-

[8] Among these historians and literary critics, George Steiner is probably the best known. See his *Language and Silence* (New York: Atheneum, 1970). See also Erich Heller, "L. Wittgenstein: Unphilosophical Notes," *Encounter,* September 1959, and *The Disinherited Mind* (New York: Meridian, 1959).

gestions are correct is far from clear. Taking the lamentations of writers like Hofmannsthal rather literally and uncritically, they have stressed the crises of the German language without troubling much to investigate the development and refinement of the language that was also going on then, precisely in ethics, aesthetics, personal relationships, the emotions. Hofmannsthal was, after all, by no means the most distinguished poet of the period. An incomparably better poet, Rainer Maria Rilke, talked rather little about the crisis of language and, instead, went about composing magnificent verse in which language is both refined and enriched.

The case of psychoanalysis is also instructive. Tending as it does to concentrate on abnormal behavior, it reflects a general tendency in most languages to develop a more refined, precise and differentiated terminology to deal with the abnormal, the deviant, the illegal, the "bad" than with what is normal, ordinary, legal, good. Words like "nice" and "good man" are indeed virtually meaningless in most contexts. In English, words like "guilt," "sin," "shame," and "vice" have no true positive counterparts, or at any rate are far more definite in their meanings than are their nearest positive counterparts, which more often indicate the absence of negative characteristics than anything definitely good. These negative terms continue to undergo modification and refinement as psychological theory develops: the distinction between guilt and shame coined by Helen Merrell Lynd and others is a good example.

As the word "good," as used in the preceding sentence, illustrates, there is also the problem that the pro-words, such as "good," "merit," "virtue"—which are likewise opposed to "bad," "demerit," "defect"—may refer to nonmoral as well as to moral values. But "evil," particularly in its adjectival sense, carries a strong, almost exclusively moral meaning, to which one can oppose on the *pro* side the much less forceful "righteous" and "virtuous" or even "good," the latter being the most general pro-word. *On the whole*, then, with some exceptions, language tends to fuse pro-words, but to differentiate among various con-words. Thus the significance of moral evil is cast into higher relief.[9]

What I want to suggest in mentioning these matters is that much of what has been written about a linguistic crisis in the German-speaking countries is grossly overdramatized, making its case by oversimplification and an almost studied neglect of the sort of obvious counterexample that I have been citing: cases where language has been refined and improved rather than debased. If one focuses one's attention on particular writers, on certain philosophers such as Martin Heidegger, and on certain literary critics such as the ones mentioned and then embellishes one's account with some examples from the propaganda of two world wars, the rise of the popular press, and the street chatter of Vienna at a time when it was still the capital city of a multilingual empire, one crudely distorts the history of the German language.

Paul Engelmann and others have claimed that Wittgenstein's attitude toward language was not only representative of the developments discussed here but was also typically Jewish. But contrast these two quotations, the

[9] Aurel Kolnai has made a special study of this phenomenon in his fine essay, "The Thematic Primacy of Moral Evil," *The Philosophical Quarterly*, January 1956.

first from a British historian, the second from a German Jewish philosopher. "Despite his repudiation of Judaism," writes Frank Field concerning Karl Kraus,

his vision of language was, in the final analysis, *rooted in the specifically Judaic concept of the* revelation of the will of God through the word, the Word of power which brings what it says to pass.[10]

On the other hand, Franz Rosenzweig writes:

There is nothing in a deeper sense Jewish than a final mistrust in the power of the Word and an inner confidence in the power of silence.[11]

Which generalization about the Jewish concept of the power of the Word is correct? *Neither.* Nor was there a catastrophic collapse of the German language at the turn of the twentieth century.

## VI

So far, in order to try to make some sense of what Wittgenstein himself described as the main point of his *Tractatus*, I have drawn attention to the so-called crisis that some persons suppose the German language to have undergone during the early part of this century, with

[10] Quoted from Frank Field, *The Last Days of Mankind: Karl Kraus and His Vienna* (London: Macmillan, 1967). My italics.

[11] Frank Rosenzweig, *Stern der Erlösung,* quoted in "Das Porträt: Ludwig Wittgenstein zur 80. Wiederkehr seines Geburtstages," Österreichische Rundfunk Studio Tirol, 1969.

particular attention to those of Wittgenstein's Viennese contemporaries who hailed, deplored and recorded this crisis, imaginary or real. When put in this Viennese setting, the *Tractatus* does make somewhat better sense.

Yet in one all-important respect Wittgenstein's work remains radically set apart from that of his Austrian contemporaries. Although Wittgenstein was to write beautifully in the German language, even to be hailed as a creator of a new style, he was by profession or avocation not a writer but a mathematician and logician—so much so that, when he voiced his own opinions on the limitations of language, he chose a different medium. Although his medium gave his work a power and scope that his literary contemporaries lacked, it also lent his views a technical and esoteric air that distracted attention from their practical inspiration and concern. I have in mind, of course, that Wittgenstein couched his own critique of language in the framework of Frege's logical theories and a variant of Russell's logical atomism.

Thus his message was to be misunderstood twice over. To his English readers, who had only a vague inkling, if any, of German linguistic crises, he was to appear as a brilliant critic of speculative philosophy—*but in the British tradition*. It had been German-inspired philosophizing in England against which G. E. Moore and Russell had directed their own analytical attack, and Wittgenstein, their student, was assumed to be working not only on the same lines but within the same limits. English readers missed Wittgenstein's wider role as a critic not only of the language of speculative philosophy but of the language of art and the emotions in the Viennese manner of Hofmannsthal. Nor did Wittgenstein fare better among his compatriots. To those Austrians and Germans who noticed him at all, he appeared as one quite foreign to the Viennese tradition of critique of language, as one who had assimilated the alien approach and techniques of British empiricism. The first among his fellow Austrians to take serious note of his philosophy were the philosopher-physicists and mathematicians of the Vienna Circle, a rather Anglophile group more interested in British empiricism and in Russell's new logic than in traditional Austrian and German philosophy. Only since Wittgenstein's death have Austrian and German litterateurs shown any interest in his work.

## VII

When one turns from the question of the several motives behind Wittgenstein's composition of the *Tractatus* to attempt to comprehend the actual content of the work, it is necessary to explain something of the nature of logical paradoxes and the renewed research into the foundations of logic and mathematics which they occasioned during the first decades of the twentieth century.

Numerous logical paradoxes exist—those of Russell, J. Richard, and Kurt Grelling, for example, as well as the classical paradoxes—of which only a few illustrative examples need be given here. The best-known is commonly referred to as the Liar Paradox, where the perpetual liar reports: "I am now lying." If what he says is true, he is speaking falsely; and if what he says is false, he is speaking truly.

Another way to put this paradox, due to Jan Lukasiewicz and Alfred Tarski,[12] is thus:

> The boxed sentence is false.

If the sentence thus boxed is true, then it is false; if it is false, then it is true.

These are peculiar utterances, and it is hardly surprising that some philosophers and logicians, when confronted by them, have wanted to declare them somehow illegitimate, neither true nor false, but ungrammatical, improperly formed—meaningless. Russell took such an approach after his discovery in 1901 of the paradoxes that can be generated from certain long-accepted ways of constructing classes or sets. Russell with his theory of types (or categories), W. V. Quine with his method of stratification, as well as other logicians, tried to avoid paradoxes or antinomies by introducing certain grammatical and logical conventions prohibiting the construction of such antinomies. The aim was to show, through logical analysis, that wherever the required grammatical and logical precautions were not being taken, one's system was in danger of producing statements or formulae which were not *well formed*, which were meaningless. Even before Russell, it had been observed that many of the antinomies were produced by their self-referential or reflexive character, and the question had been posed—for example, by Lewis Carroll (the Reverend C. L. Dodgson)—

[12] Alfred Tarski, "The Concept of Truth in Formalized Languages," in Tarski, *Logic, Semantics, Metamathematics* (Oxford, 1956), pp. 157 ff.

whether such self-reference ought not to be prohibited.[13] Specific, conflicting techniques for dealing with self-reference have since been worked out by logicians, among them Russell, Ernst Zermelo, John von Neumann, and Quine.

In these circumstances it is in a certain sense laudable, even if the conclusion is incorrect, that some philosophers have supposed that techniques rather like those developed by Russell and others for isolating meaningless from meaningful, non-well-formed from well-formed, utterances could be extended *beyond* logic to the traditional problems of philosophy. It has been supposed that the ancient problems of metaphysics, like the *logical* paradoxes, could be made to disappear through the development of canons of meaningfulness and well-formed utterance; that indeed these hoary metaphysical theories had arisen in the first place only because of the absence of techniques of linguistic and logical analysis for ascertaining meaninglessness.

This project, ambitious and inspired, was doomed to failure. For it is a fact that the self-reference which is to be found in the logical antinomies is *simply absent* from most of the traditional problems of philosophy. The failure of the project was, however, not foreseen. The story of much twentieth-century philosophy, conspicuously that of Wittgenstein and his followers, is that of an attempt to dissolve traditional metaphysics through the systematic application of a false parallel: the assumption

[13] See W. W. Bartley III, "Lewis Carroll's Unpublished Work in Symbolic Logic," *Abstracts* of the 4th International Congress for Logic, Methodology and Philosophy of Science, Bucharest, 1971, p. 416; and W. W. Bartley III, "Lewis Carroll's Lost Book on Logic," *The Scientific American*, July 1972, pp. 38–46.

that philosophical problems were generated, and could be avoided, in a way parallel to that in which logical paradoxes were generated and resolved.

Thus Wittgenstein declared bluntly in the Preface to the *Tractatus*, "The book deals with the problems of philosophy, and shows . . . that the reason why these problems are posed is that the logic of our language is misunderstood" (page 3).

## VIII

In providing a theory of demarcation between science and nonscience, Wittgenstein's *Tractatus* prescribes criteria that must be satisfied by any factual (not logical) utterances which are well-formed, and proscribes, in the several senses discussed above, utterances which do not satisfy these criteria. Factual propositions are well-formed scientific propositions. No other propositions exist, although there exist certain pseudopropositions—typically to be found in philosophy—which superficially look like propositions but which prove on analysis not to be well-formed. Wittgenstein himself does not use the locution "well-formed"; he speaks of propositions which are *meaningful* and pseudopropositions which are *meaningless*.

When confronted by a sentence whose meaningfulness may be questioned, something that may happen often since "language disguises thought" (4.002), the *Tractatus* specifies what *must* be the case if it is in fact meaningful. Leaving aside pseudopropositions for the moment, we find specified in the *Tractatus* two separate and different sorts of *legitimate* meaningful propositions.

These are atomic propositions and molecular propositions. A sentence which proves to be neither is in fact no proposition at all: it is meaningless.

Elementary, or atomic, propositions, into which all molecular propositions may be analyzed, are those propositions that derive their meaning from their direct relation to the world. Elementary propositions are themselves unanalyzable and logically independent one from the other. Very important, such an elementary proposition pictures a *possible* state of affairs in the world. If that state of affairs in fact obtains, the elementary proposition is true; if not, it is false.

So far, one might think oneself to be concerned entirely with the theory of language. In fact, an ontology, or theory of the nature and structure of reality, accompanies the linguistic theory. Wittgenstein sets out to answer the question: what has to be the case in order for there to be meaningful utterances? Part of his account of language emphasizes that the nature of the ultimate constituents of the world may be discovered by an examination of language, and the structure of language in turn is determined by the structure of reality. Wittgenstein does not restrict himself to some *particular* language here; rather, what is involved is the essential, if hidden, structure that has to be possessed by *any* language capable of meaningful expression.

In his view, the world is composed of *objects arranged as facts*. A true elementary proposition pictures such a fact, called an *atomic fact*, and such facts are, like the elementary propositions which picture them, independent one from the other. An elementary proposition may be meaningful without being true if it pictures a possible combination of objects (a state of affairs) which does not happen to obtain. Elementary propositions and the states of affairs that they picture have a common form.

Readers of the *Tractatus*—including, conspicuously, most of the logical positivists—have often supposed that elementary propositions report sense experiences. It is probably safe to assume that Wittgenstein did have, and must have had, *some* such idea in mind. But the *Tractatus* makes no declaration on this point. In his account of elementary propositions, atomic facts, and objects, Wittgenstein gives no examples; indeed, he does not even specify the *kind* of example that would qualify. It is not even stated *directly* that his objects must be *objects of human knowledge*, only that objects must exist in order for language to exist. The *Tractatus* is, then, a work in logic and ontology, not in the theory of knowledge. Ironically, Bertrand Russell is often blamed for having furthered the notion that the *Tractatus* is an epistemological work, although Russell himself, in his famous Introduction to it, wrote: "It is not contended by Wittgenstein that we can actually isolate the simple or have empirical knowledge of it. It is a logical necessity demanded by theory." (page xiii)

Fortunately, this misunderstanding of the *Tractatus* has been corrected in recent years. Professor G. E. M. Anscombe, for instance, has shown that Wittgenstein's *Tractatus* could not have involved a theory of sense-data.[14] Unfortunately, just as this misunderstanding has been eradicated, another misunderstanding has begun to

[14] G. E. M. Anscombe, *An Introduction to Wittgenstein's Tractatus* (London: Hutchinson University Library, 1959).

emerge: namely, that the *Tractatus* is dominated by Kantian themes and is indeed more Kantian than empiricist in character, despite its outward dress and its most common interpretation in English and American philosophical circles. I have already alluded to this tendency above in my critical remarks about Quinton's interpretation of the goal of the *Tractatus*. Here it may be useful, in a corrective way, to note that one of the central components of the doctrine of the *Tractatus* is not only *non*-Kantian but *pre*-Kantian in spirit. I have in mind the doctrine that the nature of the world is to be discovered through the examination and analysis of language. Before Kant it was commonly assumed that some sort of harmony existed between the human mind and the external world so that the human mind could (in some accounts even unaided by the senses) apprehend the nature of reality. Should it fail to do so, this would often, in pre-critical philosophy, be attributed to some interference with the proper functioning of the human reason. When properly functioning, the human reason has access to the nature of reality.

Kant rejected this notion, conceiving the laws of rationality not as mirroring the structure of things in themselves, which was indeed *unknowable* to man, but as providing the "forms of human understanding." Insofar as man could know reality at all, he would have to know it in accordance with these forms of human understanding. But the study of the human mind would *not* reveal the nature of reality, the *Ding an sich*.

By contrast, the common pre-Kantian view had held that "the mind itself is, in effect, a mirror that reflects without distortion the indwelling structure of the external world." [15] Wittgenstein might have said: "Language it-self is, in effect, a mirror that—when well formed—re-flects without distortion the indwelling structure of the external world." If one bears this aspect of Wittgenstein's thought in mind, it appears that the Kantian interpreta-tion of the early Wittgenstein is wrong. To be sure, there are some traces of Kantian themes there, but they in no way predominate.[16] One can find a Kantian flavor in his remark, for instance, that just as one cannot imagine spatial objects outside space or temporal objects outside time, one could not imagine an object excluded from the possibility of combining with others.

My view, which I shall mention but not explain, since to explain it would require a treatise in itself, is this. It is *more* accurate, if also a bit misleading, to argue that the movement from the early Wittgenstein to the work of the later Wittgenstein is a movement from a precritical, pre-Kantian position to a post-Kantian, Hegelian-style position *without benefit of Kant.*

## IX

Before turning from Wittgenstein's early work, as repre-sented in the *Tractatus*, to the important period in his life during which he withdrew publicly from philosophy

[15] Henry David Aiken, *The Age of Ideology* (New York: Mentor Books, 1956), p. 31.

[16] As James Griffin has pointed out, "There is no possi-bility that 'the world' can be read as 'the world of my experi-ence'; he [Wittgenstein] means, he says, reality." See James Griffin, *Wittgenstein's Logical Atomism* (Seattle: University of Washington paperbacks, 1964), p. 150.

and reshaped his philosophical outlook, three other components of the doctrine of the *Tractatus* need to be mentioned briefly: Wittgenstein's theory of complex propositions; his idea of the logical, truth-functional scaffolding of language; and his famous doctrine of "showing."

So far, only that part of scientific meaningful discourse that is expressed in elementary propositions has been discussed. Most propositions with which one deals in ordinary life and in science, however, are, according to Wittgenstein's account, not elementary propositions but complex, molecular propositions which may be analyzed into *truth-functions* of elementary propositions, and which thus owe their own meaning, and their truth value, to the elementary propositions from which they are generated. To pursue an analysis in particular cases might be difficult, but *if* the compound proposition in question is truly meaningful, such a translation can be carried out: all meaningful languages have a uniform logical structure.

The phrases "truth-function" and "logical structure" need to be explained. To say that a complex proposition can be analyzed into a truth-function of elementary propositions is to claim that it can be analyzed into a set of elementary propositions *structurally linked* by means of certain logical terms. These logical terms, which include negation and conjunction, are themselves *nondescriptive*; they are rather like structural scaffolding on which propositions are arranged; they themselves stand for nothing in the world. Thus, if we were to suppose that the letters $p$ and $q$, taken individually, stand for elementary propositions, then "$p$ and $q$" would stand for a compound proposition in which the elementary components $(p, q)$ are joined by the truth-functional connective of *conjunction* ("and"). Similarly, "neither $p$ nor $q$"

would be a compound proposition whose elementary propositional components are joined by the truth-functional connectives of *negation* and *conjunction*.

## X

Wittgenstein repeatedly and unequivocally asserted that what could not be stated in a meaningful proposition could not be stated at all. He did allow, however, that certain things which could *not* be stated in propositions were nonetheless *manifest* in meaningful propositions, wherein they *showed* themselves. Thus, some of what cannot be *said* may be *shown*.

In correspondence with Russell, Engelmann, and others, Wittgenstein several times maintained that his "doctrine of showing" was the main point of the *Tractatus*. There is little doubt that Wittgenstein did regard the doctrine as important; nonetheless, it is an aspect of the book that has had insufficient attention, owing in part to the fact that Wittgenstein himself says so little about the matter and that what he does say is highly condensed and allusive.

The best attempt to make good sense of this difficult idea has, I believe, been made by James Griffin,[17] who rightly sets the doctrine in the context of Wittgenstein's logical theory and his developments and criticisms of the views concerning logic set forth by Frege and Russell. As Griffin puts it, Wittgenstein's doctrine is in part a development of the views concerning the definition of concepts set down in Frege's *Grundgesetze*, in part a reaction to Russell's theory of types, and in part the result

[17] Griffin, *op. cit.*

of Wittgenstein's own reflection about the unique character of the propositions of logic. Thus logical controversy provides the *core* context in terms of which the theory must be understood. Wittgenstein does, however, extend the notion far beyond this core of logic in order to help him convey his views on ethics, aesthetics, and religion.

Elaborating on his view that a proposition is a picture, Wittgenstein insists that a picture cannot depict its own pictorial form—in this case a form dictated by logic. For the logical, or formative, constants are not descriptive. Nonetheless, a pictorial proposition can *display* or *show* or *make manifest* its logical structure (and the structure of the world which it pictures). Part of the import of this doctrine, if it were correct, would be to render Russell's theory of types both impossible and superfluous. By attempting to speak of such terms as "thing," "property," "fact," and "type," Russell's theory attempts to do what cannot be done even in its own terms and, in Wittgenstein's way of speaking, tries to say what cannot be said. To correct this, however, it is not necessary, so he believes, to revise the theory of types, but rather to understand, through the distinction between saying and showing, that such a theory, even if it were *per impossibile* possible, is superfluous. Wittgenstein thought that to know the sense of a symbol, definitely and completely, is to know all its possible combinations; that is, *one would know its range of applicability and thus not need a theory of types,* since to know the range of applicability of a symbol is to know its type. And if one knows its range of applicability, one will run no risk of generating logical paradox by extending it beyond its range or type.

So: one need not attempt, impossibly, to *state* or to say what the range of applicability of a symbol is; this will be shown in the symbolism if that symbolism is fully and definitely understood. And thus the emphasis put by Wittgenstein in the *Tractatus* on precisely determinate, complete definition.

This notion, although difficult to explain nontechnically, is indisputably ingenious. Russell's own great respect for the *Tractatus* stemmed in large part from this portion of the book, even though Russell himself, in his Introduction, carefully records his disbelief in the solution, summarizing his appreciation of Wittgenstein in this way: "To have constructed a theory of logic which is not at any point obviously wrong is to have achieved a work of extraordinary difficulty and importance" (page xxii).

When Russell wrote his Introduction, in May 1922, Wittgenstein's logical theory was indeed not obviously wrong. By the middle 1930s, however, his basic assumptions (as well as many of Russell's) had been completely undercut by the work of Kurt Gödel and Alonzo Church. In paragraph 6.5 of the *Tractatus*, Wittgenstein had flatly declared: "The riddle does not exist. If a question can be framed at all, it is also *possible* to answer it." Gödel's results, published in 1931, show that every arithmetical system containing addition, multiplication, and prime numbers contains *undecidable* statements or equations. For instance, given any proof procedure whatever for elementary number theory, Gödel demonstrates that a statement of elementary number theory can be constructed which will be true if, and only if, it is not provable by the proof procedure given. Thus, either the statement is provable, in which case it is false and the proof procedure used discredited, or else the statement is true but not provable. But in that case the proof procedure is *incomplete*.[18] Gödel's work, in combination with further results achieved by Alonzo Church and S. C. Kleene, has produced the added result that every *disproof* technique, however intricate it may be, leaves the nonvalidity of some nonvalid theorems undiscoverable in principle.[19] Riddles exist.

Wittgenstein's logical theory, in particular his attempt to avoid difficulties in the theory of types through a distinction between what may be said and what shown, is no longer taken seriously by logicians, nor was it at any time very influential. His extension of the doctrine of showing from logic to ethics, aesthetics, and religion is not only very brief, taking up only about six pages of the *Tractatus*, but is also largely metaphorical, even though the metaphorical character of the extension is not declared and might well have been denied by him. Thus he indicates that value, *like logic*, pervades the world and may be conveyed or shown through the meaningful propositions that may be said, whereas to attempt to say what is valuable or right leads to nonsense.

Engelmann has provided us with one good, documented example of the sort of thing Wittgenstein was trying, even if obscurely and unsuccessfully, to convey.

[18] Kurt Gödel, "Über formal unentscheidbare Sätze der Principia Mathematica und verwandter Systeme," *Monatshefte für Mathematik und Physik*, vol. 38, 1931, pp. 173–98.

[19] S. C. Kleene, "Recursive Predicates and Quantifiers," *Transactions of the American Mathematical Society*, vol. 53, 1943, pp. 41–73; Alonzo Church, "A note on the Entscheidungsproblem," *Journal of Symbolic Logic*, vol. 1, 1936, pp. 40–41, 101–2.

During the war, at Wittgenstein's request, Engelmann sent him a copy of Uhland's poem, "Graf Eberhard's Hawthorn." Engelmann says of the poem: "Each one of Uhland's verses was simple—not ingenuous, but tersely informative. . . . But the poem as a whole gives in 28 lines the picture of a life." [20]

Wittgenstein wrote back: "The poem by Uhland is really magnificent. And this is how it is: if only you do not try to utter what is unutterable then *nothing* gets lost. But the unutterable will be—unutterably—*contained* in what has been uttered!"

## XI

Helpful as such evidence is in better understanding Wittgenstein's application of his doctrine of showing to ethics, aesthetics, and religion, the best—and perhaps the only proper—way to explain the notion may be to recount some of the events of his own life during the twenties, immediately before and after the publication of the *Tractatus*, when he was teaching elementary school in lower Austria. The next chapter attempts this task and, in so doing, tries to bridge the gap between the views of the *Tractatus* and those of the later *Philosophical Investigations*.

[20] Paul Engelmann, *op. cit.*, pp. 84–85.

# 3

## NOT MADE TO MEASURE

回 回 回

*Wittgenstein was an ascetic. Such men are taken to be crazy, but one just oughtn't to measure them by ordinary standards.*

—Oskar Fuchs, Shoemaker of Trattenbach [1]

*At the present time, shoemakers, who make shoes to measure, deal more rationally with individuals than our teachers and schoolmasters in their application of moral principles.*

—Otto Weininger [2]

*I*

During the six years that Ludwig Wittgenstein spent teaching elementary school in lower Austria "the people were astonished at his doctrine: For he taught them as one having authority, and not as the scribes."

The passage just quoted is of course taken from the New Testament, and it would be possible to fit this segment of Wittgenstein's life into the framework of a morality play whose *leitmotivs* echo those of the Gospels.

[1] The late Herr Fuchs made this remark to Frau Luise Hausmann, teacher of English in Kirchberg am Wechsel, and it is recorded in her manuscript, "Wittgenstein als Volks-schullehrer," an abridged version of which is published in *Club Voltaire*, Vol. IV (Hamburg: Rowohlt Verlag, 1970), pp. 391–96, as an appendix to my essay, "Die österreichische Schulreform als die Wiege der modernen Philosophie."
[2] Otto Weininger, *Sex and Character* (London: William Heinemann, 1906), p. 57.

Almost all one would need for such a presentation is there: teaching the scribes in the temple; the call; the temptation; the life in the wilderness; the abandonment of the world and its comforts; the formation of a band of disciples; care for the poor, the meek, the peacemakers and the persecuted; the devotion to children; the working of miracles; and the healing of the sick. And there is also the antagonism of the elders, the betrayal, the trial, and rejection by the populace.

Yet we know both too little and too much about his life as a schoolmaster to cast the events of these years into such a mold. Moreover, although Wittgenstein had, as Bertrand Russell put it, "the pride of Lucifer," he also had a deep humility that any such comparison would have offended. Still, one might bear in mind several things: first, the experience to which the Gospels testify is, in one sense of the word, archetypal, and may thus be repeated without sacrilege in different ways in various times and circumstances; second, Wittgenstein had been overwhelmed by Tolstoy's version of the Gospels after reading it in Galicia in early 1915, and he had reread the Gospels countless times since then, so that, as his friends testify, he could recite large parts by heart; finally, an attempt to put something like the Sermon on the Mount, as rendered by Tolstoy, into practice is to show rather than say something. That Wittgenstein was, either consciously or unconsciously, for better or for worse, engaging in an imitation of Christ is a possibility that cannot lightly be dismissed when one attempts to comprehend his extraordinary life in Trattenbach, Puchberg, and Otterthal between 1920 and 1926. Since it is, however, only a possibility and one whose correctness would be impossible to establish or even seriously to test, it is in the spirit of Wittgenstein's philosophy to do no more than note it and for the rest to be silent, permitting the facts to speak for themselves.

There are other reasons, too, for caution in forcing any pattern, however appropriate, on these years in Wittgenstein's life. Aspects of his behavior, such as his sexual behavior or lack of it, might indeed, conveniently and perhaps correctly, be set into some pattern. The six years as a whole, however, lend themselves to no such treatment. Even if he was, in his experiences in the villages, attempting something like an imitation of Christ, he was not doing only that. For him to do that would at the same time be to essay an acting out of his own ethical position, as sketched in the *Tractatus* and in his *Notebooks*—itself an important experiment. Yet under no stretch of the imagination was Wittgenstein engaged only in ethical activity and practical philosophy during these years; he was, throughout the twenties, developing and revising some of the most technical aspects of his philosophy. Those who suppose that he dropped philosophy during this period only to be suddenly catapulted back into it again—through, for instance, attending a lecture by the Dutch mathematician L. E. J. Brouwer in March 1928—are misinformed. Again, Wittgenstein was, in a manner he was not to repeat, a *participant*, acting throughout these six years in the Austrian school-reform program. Here too he did not simply follow; he innovated educationally in an individual way that was to influence his technical philosophy. All these activities worked together, and sometimes against one another, in a convoluted way.

## II

Both Wittgenstein's *Brown Book*, dictated in 1934–35, and the first part of his *Philosophical Investigations*, in which the core of his later philosophy is brought to its most finished statement, criticize an account of how a child acquires language attributed by Wittgenstein to Saint Augustine and discernable in the writings of many philosophers. In 1926 Wittgenstein published a "Word-book" for schoolchildren.[3] And in *Zettel* (412) he asks bluntly of himself:

"Am I doing child psychology?"

It comes, then, as no surprise to learn that one story he used to tell his elementary school pupils in Trattenbach as early as 1921 goes like this:

Once upon a time there was an experiment. Two small children who had not yet learnt to speak were shut away with a woman who was unable to speak. The aim of the experiment was to determine whether they would learn some primitive language or invent a new language of their own. The experiment failed.

This story—or rather, the original version of which this can hardly be more than a partly remembered fragment —Wittgenstein recited to his nine- and ten-year-old schoolchildren during his first year of teaching. Some forty-eight years later, one of those students, now a farmer in Trattenbach, volunteered it to me as one of

[3] Ludwig Wittgenstein, *Wörterbuch für Volksschulen* (Vienna: Hölder-Pichler-Tempsky A.G., 1926).

the things he had learned, and remembered, from Wittgenstein. In this brief tale are not simply anticipated, but imbedded, some of the central concerns about language learning, primitive language, and private languages that were to preoccupy the "later Wittgenstein," who is commonly supposed to have emerged during the early thirties.

What is surprising is that Wittgenstein's six years as an elementary schoolteacher, during which he had sustained daily contact with children and was already engaged in the questions that dominate his later philosophy, are still—some twenty years after his death—cloaked in darkness. Philosophers appear to have supposed them unworthy of serious investigation. Accounts of Wittgenstein's life and work usually pass over them in a few sentences or a paragraph; rarely are even the correct dates and the right names and locations of the villages given; what information is presented is usually drawn at first or second hand from the official reports which the school authorities in Neunkirchen drew up in response to written inquiries from F. A. von Hayek (a second cousin to Wittgenstein, once removed) and others shortly after his death. These official reports, widely circulated among those interested in Wittgenstein, were prepared with little care and consist largely in uninterpreted and sometimes misleading anecdotes. One British scholar has visited the villages, but the villagers report that he consulted only officials and schoolteachers and one former pupil of Wittgenstein's (now dead) who was known to possess a letter from him. Engelmann had planned to discuss this part of Wittgenstein's life, but died before reaching that

section of his Memoir.[4] Others, while not making light
of Wittgenstein's years as a schoolmaster, pass over them
in hurried bewilderment, as if they constituted an eccentric act best not dwelt upon. Thus one American ex-
positor of his thought writes:

A man of acknowledged genius, who, after knowing next
to nothing about logic and philosophy, had made important
contributions to both fields within a remarkably short period
of time, a man who could not help having a brilliant future
in one of the most sophisticated of all intellectual disciplines—this man turned his back on all that and devoted
himself to the humble task of teaching young children in
remote villages.[5]

However one cares to explain the neglect of Wittgenstein's schoolteaching experience, Wittgenstein himself was never much interested in academic careers. His
decision to become a schoolmaster was closely related to
the activities of his family immediately following the
end of the First World War. Confronted with the economically ruined strip of land now known as the Austrian Republic, the Wittgenstein family immediately engaged in wide-ranging social work. The family had a
long tradition of public service which most of its members treated, literally, as a duty. In creating the iron and
steel industry of the Danube Monarchy (most of it situated in Bohemia and thus after 1918 in the new state of
Czechoslovakia), Karl Wittgenstein had won a position

[4] See B. F. McGuinness in his Editor's Appendix to Engelmann, *op. cit.*, p. 145.
[5] George Pitcher, *The Philosophy of Wittgenstein* (Engle-
wood Cliffs: Prentice-Hall, 1964), p. 6.

in his country comparable to that of Andrew Carnegie in America and rather like that of the Krupp family in Germany; in fact, Carnegies, Krupps, Schwabs, and Wittgensteins were guests in one another's homes prior to the war. In prewar days, the Wittgensteins were prominent patrons of the arts. Gustav Mahler, Bruno Walter, Johannes Brahms, and Clara Schumann frequently visited the Palais Wittgenstein; Joseph Joachim and his quartet often played in its great salon.[6] Karl Wittgenstein also devoted himself passionately to the visual and plastic arts after his retirement from active business in the 1890s; he built the great Viennese exhibition hall, the Sezession, and patronized many important contemporary painters. In 1914, over a year after his father's death, Ludwig made his own famous gift of 100,000 Kronen to Ludwig von Ficker to aid poets and writers, explaining to Ficker that he did so according to the custom of his family.[7]

In the immediate postwar years, however, social welfare more than the arts engaged the attention of Karl Wittgenstein's children. Herbert Hoover named Margarete Stonborough his personal representative for Austria in charge of work for the American Food Relief Commission, a role which put her in close touch with socialist and other political leaders in Vienna, including, conspicuously, Otto Glöckel, who, as administrative head

[6] See Bruno Walter, *Theme and Variations: An Autobiography* (London: Hamish Hamilton, 1947).

[7] The story of Wittgenstein's relationship with Ficker has now been recounted in great detail. See Ludwig Wittgenstein, *Briefe an Ludwig von Ficker* (Salzburg: Otto Müller Verlag, 1969), including Walter Methlagl's essay, "Erläuterungen zur Beziehung zwischen Ludwig Wittgenstein und Ludwig von Ficker."

of the school-reform program, was concerned directly with the economic redevelopment of the countryside through the education and reeducation of the peasantry. Ludwig's eldest sister, Mining, opened a day school for poor Viennese boys near Grinzing, and eventually helped him with his own pupils in the countryside. In this context, Wittgenstein's decision to enter elementary school-teaching—quite apart from any philosophical importance it may eventually have acquired—was hardly eccentric.

In any event, he was only one among hundreds of newly trained and often highly talented young school-teachers, many of them returned veterans like himself, who poured out from Vienna into the Austrian countryside in September 1920. Among other talented young Austrians to enter the school-reform movement during the 1920s were Ludwig Erik Tesar, who, like Rainer Maria Rilke and Georg Trakl, had benefited from Wittgenstein's prewar bequest to Ficker, and at least two philosophers who were to become closely associated with the problems that preoccupied the members of the Vienna Circle: Karl Popper and Edgar Zilsel. The Vienna Circle itself, in its own first manifesto, associated itself with the aims of the school-reform movement.[8]

### III

What was the Austrian school-reform program? How and why did it arise? For what did it stand?

The unsatisfactory character of the prewar school

[8] *Wissenschaftliche Weltauffassung: Der Wiener Kreis* (Vienna: Artur Wolf Verlag, 1929), p. 10.

systems of Germany and Austria has been dramatically conveyed by some of the most eminent German-speaking artists and writers. One need think only of Robert Musil's *Young Törless*, Hermann Hesse's story "Beneath the Wheel," or the film *Mädchen in Uniform* to recall the themes and the mood of the protest against a repressive and counterproductive school system.

Nonetheless, the Austrians, under the Hapsburgs, had enjoyed one of the more progressive school systems in Europe—progressive, of course, only in contrast to the systems of some other European countries, including England. In itself, it was anything but a paradigm of enlightened thinking: instruction, largely in the control of the Roman Catholic Church, was authoritarian and regimented. As Count Rottenhan, imperial adviser, had defined its aims, the purpose of the lower schools was "to make thoroughly pious, good, *tractable*, and industrious men of the labouring classes of the people." The constitution of the common schools issued by the Kaiser in 1805 was unequivocal: "The method of instruction," it decreed, "must endeavour first and foremost to train the memory; then, however, according to the pressure of the circumstances, the intellect and the heart. *The trivial schools will strictly refrain from any explanations other than those exactly prescribed in the 'school and method book' . . .*" [9]

One might suppose that no educational philosophy other than expediency lay behind this approach. In fact,

[9] See Karl Strack, *Geschichte des deutschen Volksschulwesens* (Gütersloh, 1872), pp. 327–30, as quoted in Charles A. Gulick, *Austria from Habsburg to Hitler* (Berkeley and Los Angeles: The University of California Press, 1948), Vol. I, p. 546. My italics.

it was thoroughly dressed out in a philosophical psychology known as "associationism," a viewpoint that has some superficial points of similarity with Wittgenstein's early philosophy. Associationism as developed and presented in Austria derives chiefly from the views propounded by Johann Friedrich Herbart (1776–1841), whose followers filled most of the chairs of philosophy in Austria after the revolution of 1848.[10] This view takes on subtle and complicated forms, but put crudely it considers the human mind to be neutral and passive, lacking innate faculties for producing ideas. The notion that the human mind is something like a passive storehouse suited admirably the conservative social goals of Hapsburg educators. Teaching, for them, consisted in feeding students, by rote drill and association, those ideas which, so it had been decided, should dominate their lives. At no time, Herbart had argued, should a teacher engage in active debate with his students. As he explained in his *Outlines of Educational Doctrine:* "Cases may arise when the impetuosity of the pupil challenges the teacher to a kind of combat. Rather than accept such a challenge, he will usually find it sufficient at first to reprove calmly, to look on quietly, to wait until fatigue sets in." [11]

Against such a doctrine and the school system which embodied it, Otto Glöckel and his fellow reformers mounted a fierce attack, insisting that the old "drilling schools" of the Hapsburgs, as they were known, be replaced by a new kind of educational establishment,

[10] Heinrich Gomperz, "Philosophy in Austria During the Last Sixty Years," *The Personalist*, 1936, pp. 307–11.

[11] J. F. Herbart, *Outlines of Educational Doctrine* (Macmillan, 1904), p. 165.

dubbed the "Arbeitsschule," or "Working School," in which the pupil would participate *actively* in his lessons. The word "Arbeit," or "work," referred in part to the new manual training and crafts that were introduced into the curriculum in order to acquaint middle-class children with some of the real difficulties and skills involved in manual labor. But more importantly, in the context of the German phrase "sich etwas erarbeiten," it referred to an active participation in lessons, aiming no longer simply at the passive rote learning and storage of facts of the drill schools, but at the development of capabilities. "Sich etwas erarbeiten" suggests in German acquiring knowledge by working or puzzling something out for oneself. What was wanted now was more independent and original thinking, activity, on the part of students—activity, as opposed to the *fatigue* that Herbart thought would set in when a pupil dared to play an active part in his education.

The school reformers, most of whom were socialists (Social Democrats), viewed the change in orientation as politically necessary to free the future farming and working classes of the new republic from authoritarian attitudes toward learning and to fit them to participate as citizens of a democracy, actively weighing issues and deciding for themselves rather than passively accepting state decrees and church authority.

The program sounded admirable, in fact worked surprisingly well, and caught the attention of educators throughout the world. But in the semifeudal society that prevailed in much of German Austria after the First World War—outside of industrial cities such as Vienna and Graz—such an approach seemed less a program of educational reform, more a program for dissent and revolution. Ludwig Wittgenstein himself was far from being enthusiastic in his support of the program; although he and his family got to know Glöckel himself fairly well, Wittgenstein often poked fun at the reform program's more vulgar slogans and projects. Yet hardly any better illustration can be found of the potentialities as well as the dangers of school reform from a political standpoint than Wittgenstein's own experiences with it in lower Austria. The majority of the villagers among whom he lived came to regard him and his new teaching methods as dangerously threatening to their way of life.

Wittgenstein's experiences provide a good, but by no means isolated, example of this reaction. It appears from the bitter reaction to the school-reform program which occurred in the late twenties and early thirties that even run-of-the-mill school reformers were able to evoke some such response when they attempted to put reforms into effect in the Austrian countryside, for the peasant farmer forces eventually mounted a reaction to Glöckel throughout the land, first confining the reform to Vienna, and then, after the Dollfuss dictatorship of 1934 (the main support for which came from the countryside), abolishing it entirely.

Ironically, Karl Wittgenstein might have predicted such a reaction from the Austrian peasantry. Already in 1898, speaking of the importance of educating the industrial worker and the farmer, the elder Wittgenstein had written: "the uneducated peasant, who himself has learnt nothing, and does not have his son taught anything . . . is the point of departure and the greatest support for all efforts, which, partly consciously and partly unconsciously, hinder all progress." [12] Karl Wittgenstein would hardly have suspected that his son Ludwig, then only nine years old, would eventually go into the countryside to try to educate the peasantry, armed not with his father's own dim view of them but with Tolstoy's romantic vision of the noble serf in mind.

## IV

A man without expectations can hardly be disappointed; and there can be no doubt that a year in Trattenbach left Wittgenstein bitterly disappointed.

Although set in the mountains, Trattenbach is hardly one of Austria's more charming or pretty villages. Situated 2,500 feet above sea level and closed in between a steep range of mountains, reaching up to 5,000 feet, to the north and a small rivulet and further high mountains to the south, it is now an untidy, unkempt place with dreary buildings, and it must have been far drearier when Wittgenstein lived there. The climate is severe, and the steep mountains restrict the amount of sunshine reaching the villages except on those days when Trattenbach, which itself runs roughly from east to west, lies in the sun's direct path.

Yet Wittgenstein's first response to the place was almost enthusiastic. Within a week of his arrival he wrote to Bertrand Russell, then in Peking, to tell him of his new post and to report: "A short while ago I was *terribly depressed* and tired of living, but now I am slightly more

[12] Karl Wittgenstein, "The Causes of the Development of Industry in America," Vienna, privately printed and published, in English, by its author, 1898, p. 23.

hopeful." [13] Three weeks later a letter that was enthusiastic by Wittgenstein's standards went off to Engelmann: "I am working in a beautiful little nest called Trattenbach. . . . I am happy in my work at school, and I do need it badly, or else all the devils in Hell break loose inside. . . ." [14]

The about-face that Wittgenstein made during his first year in Trattenbach reminds one of several passages from one brief page of his *Tractatus*, written some years before he set foot in the village. There he had written:

Ethics and aesthetics are one and the same. . . .
If the good or bad exercise of the will does alter the world, it can alter only the limits of the world, not the facts—not what can be expressed by means of language.
In short, the effect must be that it becomes an altogether different world. It must, so to speak, wax and wane as a whole.
The world of the happy man is a different one from that of the unhappy man. [15]

It is hardly likely that Trattenbach or its people underwent any significant change—that the facts were altered—during Wittgenstein's first year there. But by the start of his second year in the village, Wittgenstein, deeply unhappy, found his "beautiful little nest" odious. Just a year after the letter to Russell quoted above, he wrote again to Russell, now returned to England, that he was "still at Trattenbach, surrounded, as ever, by odious-

[13] Quoted in Russell, *op. cit.*, Vol. II, pp. 166–67.
[14] Engelmann, *op. cit.*, pp. 38–39.
[15] Ludwig Wittgenstein, *Tractatus Logico-Philosophicus* (London: Routledge and Kegan Paul, 1961), new translation by D. F. Pears and B. F. McGuinness, propositions 6.421, 6.43.

ness and baseness. I know that human beings on the average are not worth much anywhere, but here they are much more good-for-nothing and irresponsible than elsewhere. I will perhaps stay on in Trattenbach for the present year but probably not any longer, because I don't get on well here even with the other teachers (perhaps that won't be any better in another place). . . ." [16]

Russell objected that all men are wicked, and Trattenbachers no more than others.[17] Wittgenstein, who evidently did have some difficulty in expressing himself on this matter in language, took Russell's point, replying: "You are right: the Trattenbachers are not uniquely worse than the rest of the human race. But Trattenbach is a particularly insignificant place in Austria and the *Austrians* have sunk so miserably low since the war that it's too dismal to talk about." [18]

Wittgenstein's world had evidently waned as a whole. And it had waned during the course of his moral encounter with the Trattenbachers; in the exercise of his will upon them he had altered the limits of his world.

Russell has described Wittgenstein's passionate, intense, dominating purity, while Leonard Woolf has commented on Wittgenstein's aggressively cruel streak. Russell and Woolf were well able to discriminate and weigh such traits; to the villagers of Trattenbach, whose children and grandchildren, nephews and nieces, were being

---

[16] Russell, *op. cit.*, Vol. II, pp. 167–68.
[17] *Ibid.*, p. 139.
[18] *Ibid.*, pp. 169–70. Russell ignores Wittgenstein's actual reply, even though it was printed in his own book, and fantasizes the exchange. See p. 139, and compare pp. 169–70. Many factual misstatements concerning Wittgenstein appear in Russell's book.

taught by Wittgenstein, honesty and cruelty often amounted to the same thing. Ruthless, impassioned honesty, particularly when unsolicited, can be cruelly sadistic.

A genius, Weininger writes, finds it tortuously difficult to lie. In Trattenbach and Otterthal Wittgenstein came to avoid other adults as far as possible; but when he did encounter them, he did not lie, and they hated him for it.

Many of the children, however, adored Wittgenstein. And they taught one another.

## V

What sort of people were these "good-for-nothing and irresponsible" Trattenbachers whose "wickedness" Russell had to defend? And how did they come so grievously to offend Wittgenstein?

It is hardly likely that Wittgenstein ever read E. M. Forster's ironic remark, in *Howards End*, about the very poor who "are unthinkable, and only to be approached by the statistician or the poet." Had he read it, he would surely have rejected the remark, if not the irony, outright. Wittgenstein had gone into the peasant countryside of lower Austria with a naïvely romantic notion of peasant simplicity and honesty, some of it derived from the democratic slogans of the new Austrian Republic, some from the school-reform program, some from his own experiences during the war, but most from reading Tolstoy's exaltation of "noble" peasant life. Wittgenstein's anticipation of peasant virtue was reinforced by his disgust with city life and his often voiced contempt for what he called the "half-educated" city folk corrupted by the popular press—against whom Wittgenstein, like Karl Kraus, inveighed throughout the postwar period.

One need not exaggerate Wittgenstein's romanticism. But if the poor are not unthinkable, either in Wittgenstein's or in Forster's sense, it remains true that they are, at least as individuals, not really much thought about. In his first year in Trattenbach, charged with the responsibility for their future, Wittgenstein encountered individually, and thought about, poor central European peasants with an intensity not known to Tolstoy. Perhaps what most offended him was their obstinate failure to conform to anything approaching Tolstoy's portrait. Tolstoy, in his *Confession*, had reported how, on returning from abroad, he settled in the country and occupied himself with peasant schools, wherein he was able to avoid facing what he called the "falsity" of the cities. Wittgenstein, however, *did* encounter falsity and crude veniality among the peasantry. He learned that the poor were indeed, as Forster put it, "inferior to most rich people . . . not as courteous as the average rich man, nor as intelligent, nor as healthy, nor as lovable." If many things about Wittgenstein's sojourn in the countryside are unclear, it is all too clear that, with all the famous will power of his family working in him, he refused to accept what he clearly observed— indeed, what his father had already described; and despite his denunciations of these people and his early disillusionment with them, he threw his fantastic energy and imagination into a desperate six-year-long attempt to "get the peasantry out of the muck," to cite the phrase he used again and again when explaining his goals and educational views to friends and colleagues.

In the end, Wittgenstein's radical effort to reform the peasantry—even the few thousand that he encountered in three small villages—failed miserably. Not only did those he tried to help reject him, but they eventually ran him out of town. On the other hand, his effort may have succeeded in a way of which he never became aware. For Wittgenstein did have a profound effect on the peasant children whom he taught, and they on him. Moreover, one need not disagree with Forster to maintain that poor *children* are often superior in many ways to most rich *adults:* that they are more intelligent, more healthy, more lovable, and in their own way more courteous, than rich adults—rich *adults*, not rich children. During his life Wittgenstein taught only two sorts of person: the privileged adults who were his students and colleagues at Cambridge and poor Austrian peasant children. His later philosophy suggests that he learned as much, and probably more, from those children than he learned from adults.

The some three dozen children with whom he had to deal directly in Trattenbach formed only a tiny fraction of the village's population. In 1920 some 800 persons lived there. By contrast to many Austrian mountain villages—including neighboring Otterthal, a farming community—Trattenbach was not homogeneous. A factory, a wool mill, had been established there, and some 200 inhabitants labored in it; most of the rest of the population, apart from a few village tradesmen such as the grocer and shoemaker, were engaged in farming.

In addition to reporting the size of the village and the distribution of its population, the statistician can confirm that it was indeed miserable: both farms and factories were in desperate shape right after the war. The Trattenbachers were undernourished; they were anxious and harassed by their condition; and democracy for them at first meant not independence but separation. Within the village a kind of class conflict already existed, separating workers and farmers—and their children—from one another. The reasons were not strictly economic: workers were sometimes better off than farmers, yet the farmers enjoyed a certain social status denied the workers. Projecting their internal troubles on the tiny mountain area surrounding them, the Trattenbachers proceeded to break away from their ancient economic and administrative unit: until 1923 Trattenbach had been united administratively with the neighboring communities of Kranichberg and Otterthal, but after some five years of bickering, Trattenbach, poorest of the three, managed to break away—and to remain poorest.

Besides the indigenous villagers, a tiny outside elite lived or exerted its influence in Trattenbach: the village priest represented the presence and power of the Church; the village schoolmasters, including Wittgenstein, the presence of the State. Through the factory, outside economic interest was represented too. A certain Herr Mautner—of whom it is now remembered only that he was owner or part owner of the factory (now closed), that he was Jewish, that he had land and servants in the area, and that Ludwig Wittgenstein flatly refused to meet him despite repeated invitations—also resided in the village. Mautner does not enter into this story; but the village priest and schoolmasters, and their district superiors, do play an important role.

Among the latter, the most important was Wilhelm

Kundt. He was not a Trattenbacher, but as District School Superintendent he figures importantly in any attempt to reconstruct school life in Neunkirchen, the large countryside school district in lower Austria which embraces all three of the elementary schools where Wittgenstein taught from 1920 to 1926. From what can be learned about Kundt, it can be established that Neunkirchen, unlike a large part of the countryside, was from the outset of the first Austrian Republic a district in which Glöckel's school reforms were being implemented. Kundt had come to Neunkirchen, full of the slogans of school reform, in 1919, a year before Wittgenstein arrived, and he remained superintendent there until 1933 when, during a period of drastic upheaval in Austria's educational programs, he was transferred to Mödling, near Vienna, and replaced after a few months by an opponent of school reform. Kundt is known to have achieved considerable success in implementing Glöckel's program in his district; as late as 1929, when the tide, in the Austrian countryside as a whole, had already turned strongly against the reform movement, visiting study commissions from such places as Carinthia turned in surprised reports about Kundt's success in reforming the schools of his district in line with Glöckel's principles.[19] Whether Kundt had had anything to do with bringing Wittgenstein to Neunkirchen is unknown, but for nearly six years he supported him, persuaded him to stay in the district, and attempted to soothe his relations with some of the villagers.

[19] Willibald Schneider, "100 Jahre Reichsvolksschulgesetz und Schulaufsicht im Schulbezirk Neunkirchen," in *Erziehung und Unterricht*, Vienna, May 1969, pp. 329–38.

Already at Trattenbach before either Kundt or Wittgenstein arrived were two other schoolteachers, Georg Berger and Martin Scherleitner, both of whom had been assigned to Trattenbach in 1918. Both had missed formal training in school-reform principles, but Scherleitner, an energetic and intelligent man, picked up the new ideas and endorsed some of them strongly. The reform appears to have meant little if anything to Berger, a pathetically dull man. Three other teachers who came and went while Wittgenstein was there need not be mentioned here. Even Scherleitner was not stationed constantly at Trattenbach during this period, but went back and forth to Otterthal and other schools in the district. In effect, the school was run by Wittgenstein and Berger, and the latter in time became principal.

With Kundt and Scherleitner, Wittgenstein maintained good relations; Berger and another man who remained at Trattenbach only one term are those about whom Wittgenstein complained in his letter to Russell.

Wittgenstein's only genuine friendship in either Trattenbach or Otterthal, however, was with Father Alois Neururer, the parish priest. A petulant romantic like Wittgenstein, Neururer had arrived in Trattenbach in 1917. A rebel innovator, and a "long-haired socialist" to boot, Neururer was concerned less in providing the traditional comforts of religion than in effecting religious and moral awakening among the members of his flock. When one of the villagers, on his deathbed, refused the last rites of the Church and expressed his contempt for it, Neururer went about expressing his admiration for the man. When his conduct of the Mass was challenged (he often used German rather than Latin, and conducted

Mass facing the congregation, liturgical practices which were of course approved for general use by the Roman Catholic Church only after Vatican Council II), Neururer calmly proclaimed to his parishioners that he could do anything that the Pope could do. From his pulpit, Neururer would abuse the people of the village mercilessly. When Arvid Sjögren came to visit Wittgenstein, as he did regularly, the two would gleefully go to church together—although neither was Roman Catholic—to listen to Neururer berate the Trattenbachers. Neururer was finally run out of Trattenbach in 1936.

In the early twenties Neururer and Wittgenstein found themselves allied in their efforts to reform the adult community of Trattenbach. Although kindred personalities in some respects, in an important way the two differed and complemented one another. Wittgenstein could rarely relax with adults outside his family, not even with those he knew well. Army records of him, while describing him as a "good comrade," also comment on his "shyness"; similarly, the adult Trattenbachers encountered only an aloof awkwardness from him that came across as gruffness. Toward the schoolchildren alone was Wittgenstein able to show affection and tenderness. Neururer, by contrast, although ineffectual with children, was able to show affectionate understanding as well as harsh discipline toward the adult villagers. So the Catholic priest deferred to Wittgenstein in teaching, even in religious instruction, whereas Wittgenstein used Neururer as his agent, in effect, in quite ordinary transactions with the townspeople.

To perform one of his most famous deeds in Trattenbach, his "miracle"—or rather, a miracle in the eyes of the villagers—Wittgenstein had to call on the good offices of both Berger and Neururer. I have in mind the well-known story of the time the steam engine in the wool factory stopped. Engineers called in from Vienna, at a loss to repair it, recommended, to the dismay of director and workers, that it be dismantled and returned to Vienna for repair. Since this would have meant a temporary closing of the factory, Wittgenstein asked Berger to secure permission from the factory foreman to let him examine the machine. After this request was reluctantly granted, Wittgenstein appeared at the factory, accompanied by Berger, examined the machine from all sides, and then requested the aid of four workmen. In accordance with Wittgenstein's directions, the workmen tapped the machine in rhythm and, to the astonishment of those present, it began to work. Wittgenstein refused the proffered payment but, when pressed, agreed to let the factory give Neururer woolen cloth to distribute to the village children. Here in one incident is displayed Wittgenstein's extraordinary competence, for which he was both admired and feared, and his intense fear of rejection. He did not have the courage to approach the factory foreman himself, but needed Berger to speak up for him; nor did he dare to distribute gifts to the villagers himself, having repeatedly been rebuffed by them. This work of charity, as well as numerous others, was undertaken by Neururer on Wittgenstein's behalf.

## VI

Once, when questioned by a villager about his religion, Wittgenstein replied that although he was not a Christian, he was an "evangelist." The villager was bewildered, for Wittgenstein emphasized that he did not mean that he was a Protestant (or "Evangelical"). What Wittgenstein was trying to say cannot be determined with certainty, but it appears he intended to suggest that although his business had something to do with the saving of souls and the proclamation of a gospel, these need not take place in a formal Christian framework.

The gospel that he had to proclaim was one shown to the villagers by the form of life he adopted. His outward behavior seems to have been calculated to shock them into the awareness of different possibilities of life, to jolt them out of their prejudices, to confuse and bewilder them to a point where they, as well as their children, could learn what he had, if not to say, then to show.

The initial paradox was, of course, the presence of a man of his background in a place like Trattenbach. Wittgenstein himself was aware of and, at least at first, amused by his situation: when writing to Russell, he remarked that this was probably the first time the schoolmaster of Trattenbach had been in correspondence with the professor of philosophy in Peking. Had he wished to do so, Wittgenstein could probably have gone into Trattenbach and the other villages incognito: his family possessed enough influence in Vienna to make some such arrangement. However, he went out of his way to ensure that the villagers would know who he was, or at least that they would know of his family's wealth and influence, of his own education and aristocratic background, and of his academic achievement in England. He told his school colleagues and several villagers about the *Tractatus*: it had not yet been published, and when he first described it to them, he referred to it as a book called "Der Satz," or "The Proposition," adding that they would "not be able to understand one word of it." Shortly after his first arrival in Trattenbach, Wittgenstein was visited by Hänsel (who came to see him—as did his friends Drobil, a sculptor, and Nähr, a photographer—approximately every second month throughout his sojourn in the villages). While taking lunch together in the inn, Wittgenstein and Hänsel talked about life in Vienna in voices that the villagers present, listening intently, easily overheard. One of Wittgenstein's remarks to Hänsel which is still remembered is this: "Ich hatte einst einen Diener, der hieß Konstantin" ("I once had a servant named Konstantin"). Later during Hänsel's visit, Wittgenstein and he cornered poor Georg Berger in the school office, and Wittgenstein demanded to know what the villagers had to say about him. Berger reports that he replied reluctantly, fearing Wittgenstein's temper, "The people take you to be a rich baron." Wittgenstein was satisfied with the answer, but remarked to Berger that although he had indeed been rich, he had given all his money away to his siblings "in order to do a good deed."

Having established his background, Wittgenstein set about showing his contempt, or at least lack of concern, for the things that villagers might expect money to buy. He lived in ostentatious poverty. Father Neururer had already irritated the villagers with his long hair and shabby clothes, but at least he maintained a house and housekeeper (his sister), whereas Wittgenstein lived in a tiny and primitive room. At first he had put up in the inn, Zum braunen Hirschen, in Trattenbach; but one Friday evening not long after his arrival he stormed out in a rage at the loud and rather drunken singing of the villagers downstairs and demanded quarter that night with the Bergers. For a time after his departure from the inn, Wittgenstein slept in the school kitchen. Still later he moved into the tiny attic room over the grocery store. In Puchberg and Otterthal he was to live in even more primitive quarters.

In his dress, Wittgenstein rejected the traditional costume of the schoolmaster, hat, suit, tie and collar, in favor of a simple uniform: he wore a plain clean shirt with open collar; gray trousers; a pair of shoes for the warmer months, and boots in winter. For cold weather he wore a leather wind jacket, but during his sojourn in Trattenbach he went without a hat. Almost always he carried a bamboo walking stick and was often seen on his solitary walks with an old briefcase or a notebook tucked under his arm.

What struck the hungry villagers even more than Wittgenstein's living arrangements and dress was his diet. He took his lunch with the family Traht, one of the poorest families in the area, each afternoon. The Trahts were exceptionally simple and pious farmers, introduced to him by Neururer, and they were the only villagers to whom Wittgenstein formed any emotional attachment. Each day he made the half-hour hike up the mountain north of the village to their small house for his midday meal. Although Wittgenstein could hardly have communicated with the Trahts in a way that would have amounted to friendship, he was greatly attracted to them and is said to have been particularly impressed by their religious piety. They were the only villagers with whom he kept in contact after his departure from Neunkirchen in 1926: he sent them postcards from England, and twice during the 1930s, the last time in 1933, Wittgenstein stole secretly back to Trattenbach, in Neururer's company, to visit old Frau Traht, who had become seriously ill.

However strongly attached to this family Wittgenstein may have become, one can only speculate how poor the lunch they served him must have been; for the other villagers, whose own food was inadequate, despised the Trahts for their poverty. Wittgenstein's evening meal was no better. It consisted of cocoa and oatmeal, which he prepared for himself in his room. Sometimes he would fetch his milk from the Trahts; sometimes one of his pupils fetched it for him. Most of his best pupils took dinner with him at one time or another, and each brought home the same horrified tale. Wittgenstein used a sort of pressure cooker for heating cocoa with oatmeal and other unspecified ingredients. He never washed the pot, so that what remained became caked inside it, got harder and harder, and grew ever larger, diminishing the pot in volume. Finally the volume of the pot was so much reduced that cocoa could be prepared for only one person at a time.

## VII

Wittgenstein's undisguised disregard for their material values unnerved the villagers of Trattenbach and Otterthal. But so much they might have tolerated; they had, after all, heard of eccentric millionaires as well as religious hermits, and they put up with Neururer until

1936. What alarmed and frightened them, as well as aroused their jealousy, was Wittgenstein's relationship with their children. The conflict between image and reality, or "cognitive dissonance," involved here must have been extreme. In the course of gossiping heatedly about him, the villagers gradually built up for themselves a picture of Wittgenstein as an unbelievably cruel teacher who constantly and mercilessly beat their children. Nonetheless, they were confronted with the brute fact that their children were more than willing to spend the entire day with this "monster," long after school hours, rather than to return home to their families. Eventually the villagers resorted to the courts in an unsuccessful attempt to *prove* that Wittgenstein did beat their children sadistically.

Only Neururer appears to have been entirely immune to the alarm, fright, and simple jealousy that Wittgenstein aroused. Wittgenstein's colleague Berger, an inferior and unpopular teacher, was as threatened as were the villagers by Wittgenstein's successes with the children, so much so that Berger in effect went native in order to protect himself, spending much of his time socializing and gossiping with the villagers and stirring up hard feelings against Wittgenstein. And he did what no Austrian schoolmaster need ever have done: he began social climbing in Trattenbach, of all places, playing favorites with the richer farm children and neglecting the children of the factory workers. After Wittgenstein's departure from the area he reversed procedures that the former had initiated, and in later years, still haunted by his encounter with Wittgenstein, he sought to erase the very name of Wittgenstein from the Trattenbach school records: in the large Trattenbach chronicle published in 1934 Wittgenstein's name is conspicuously missing from the otherwise accurate list of schoolmasters who had served there.[20] Only when he heard of Wittgenstein's posthumous fame did Berger acquire friendly memories of his former colleague.

## VIII

To understand the intensity of the reaction of the Trattenbach and Otterthal villagers to Wittgenstein, a few examples of his way of dealing with his schoolchildren may be useful. To the adult villagers we know that for the most part he remained aloof; from time to time he would descend into their lives—by repairing the steam engine at the factory, for instance, or by prescribing a treatment for some illness, showing a farmer or a housewife how to mend some equipment, or sending a pair of shoes, by way of Neururer, to some poor village family. With the children he was another person entirely.

Some things that Wittgenstein could offer his pupils were of a tangible sort that any schoolmaster with some extra money could have given. He provided out of his own, or his sister Mining's, pocket extra food (fruit in particular and occasionally chocolate), and also routinely prescribed, but rarely issued, school equipment. He brought his own microscope to Trattenbach from Vienna, and in each of his schools he carefully put to-

[20] Franz Scheibenreif, *Orts- und Hauschronik von Trattenbach* (Gemeindeamt Trattenbach: Im Selbstverlag und Kommissions Verlag; Druck: K. Mühlberger, Neunkirchen, 1934).

gether, with the aid of the children, skeletons of small animals for use in the elementary zoology and nature-lore lessons. The skeleton of a cat that he assembled at Puchberg is still in use there. He also had the children help him construct models of steam engines, pulleys, and other mechanical instruments. The models that Wittgenstein and his pupils constructed were, one is told, rather better built than most of those made elsewhere at this time; but the act in itself was not unusual. During these years most village schoolmasters were being asked to construct such equipment, since school budgets could not afford professional equipment.

The excursions on which Wittgenstein took his pupils —to the printing press in Gloggnitz, and to Vienna—fall more or less into the same category. Mining and her brother covered all expenses themselves, but another schoolmaster with extra cash might have done the same. Berger, who was at this time busily borrowing money from Wittgenstein—and returning it to him after inflation had reduced its value—could not afford these outings; but they were common in Austria at this time, particularly in the cities and larger towns where travel expense was less. Outings of some sort were prescribed by the reform program.

Wittgenstein would doubtless have made adventures of these activities whether a school-reform program had existed or not; nonetheless, some of his best-known feats, often treated as peculiar exploits, were directly in line with school-reform directives. Indeed, Wittgenstein wrote up his projects and school activities by reference to these principles in the reports he was required to submit regularly to Kundt.

Identifying catchwords were attached to the main school-reform principles, two of the most important of which were *"Selbsttätigkeit,"* meaning "self-activity," and *integrated instruction*. Some sense of Wittgenstein's way of implementing these principles emerges from the stories told about the composition of his Wordbook and about the excursions to Vienna on which he led his children.

"Self-activity" designated the attempt to encourage youngsters to figure things out for themselves actively instead of being force-fed information by the teacher in the style of the pre-reform drilling school. Prior to 1919, in accordance with drill-school methodology, rules of spelling and grammar had been dictated, written on the blackboard perhaps, and then memorized by rote. After the reform, drill was dropped in favor of an attempt to encourage the children to discover the rules of spelling and grammar for themselves. First they wrote essays freely without particular attention to spelling or grammar; only after they had acquired some fluency in written expression was grammar introduced to correct what had been written. To introduce grammar as well as correct spelling, students were asked to compile word lists. Wittgenstein's own *Wörterbuch für Volksschulen,* which was published as an officially approved school textbook in 1926, was meant to aid the active learning of both spelling and grammar. He had begun to compile it, with the aid of his students, as early as 1921. Each pupil was required to prepare at home, and to bind for himself, his own wordbook containing the words he had used in his own essays. Wittgenstein, in turn, compiled a corrected master list of words, which was available in his schoolroom as the students' "dictionary." If, in the course of writing further essays, doubts arose about spelling or certain sorts of usage, the pupils could check for themselves in the wordbook to which they themselves had contributed.

In explaining his decision to publish his own wordbook, Wittgenstein would produce examples of wordbooks then in general use and show, page by page, how poorly adapted these were for teaching either spelling or grammar. They were, for instance, littered with foreign words that were not only unknown to the children but that might make a wordbook appear an awesome tool to handle. Also, in these traditional wordbooks examples of usage tended to be literary and complicated, often far too difficult for the average child to comprehend. Wittgenstein's own wordbook is distinctive in that it consists entirely of words actually used by his own pupils in their essays *and* introduces words from the dialect as well as from High German. Wittgenstein deliberately took the unorthodox step of introducing dialect in order to teach grammatical usage. People who use dialect German quite often mix up dative and accusative constructions. Therefore, to bring home to them the difference between the two cases, Wittgenstein introduced simple examples where the distinction was clear even in dialect. His method is especially clear in his presentation of the dative and accusative of the third-person pronouns:

*ihm*, "to him," a dative form, is introduced as follows: "In dialect, 'eam.' For example: 'I hob *eam* g'sogt.'" (The sentence that Wittgenstein presents here is a dialect rendering of the High German: "Ich habe ihm gesagt,' or 'I said to him.')

*ihn,* "him," an accusative form, is introduced in this way: "In dialect, 'n' or 'm.' For example: 'I hob *m* g'sehn.'" (Here Wittgenstein's example exhibits the dialect rendering of the High German sentence: 'Ich habe ihn gesehen,' or 'I saw him.')

*ihnen,* "to them," a dative plural form, Wittgenstein introduces in a similar way: "In dialect: 'eana.' For example: 'I hob 's *eana* g'sogt.'" (Here the example is a dialect rendering of the High German sentence: 'Ich habe es ihnen gesagt,' or 'I said it to them.')

Such a presentation is simple and straightforward, yet ingenious. Instead of campaigning against the use of dialect, Wittgenstein himself uses dialect in order to teach grammar!

Wittgenstein used similar step-by-step procedures and illustrations from the dialect to teach other distinctions; for example, that between the definite article *das,* "the," and the conjunction *daß,* "that."

Here, as in mathematics, Wittgenstein argued that the child should learn the principle of a thing through an *interesting,* though possibly difficult, specific case; even if other standard examples were easier to learn, there was no point in cluttering up the mind of the child with them unless he understood and could apply the principle behind them. Thus one went from the unusual to the ordinary rather than—as many teachers had hitherto supposed—from the ordinary to the unusual. When Robert Dottrens, of the Institut Jean-Jacques Rousseau in Geneva, wrote of the school-reform program: "Like the instruction in the native tongue and in writing, the teaching of arithmetic is completely changed. . . . *The meaning of the operations is discovered while their technique is being acquired"* (p. 58, my italics), he touched on the nerve of Wittgenstein's later comment in *Zettel* (412) that he was "making a connexion between the concept of teaching and the concept of meaning."

In putting together his wordbook, Wittgenstein implemented not only the school-reform principle of "self-activity" but also the reform aim that had been dubbed "integrated instruction." The second slogan designates two closely connected goals: the teacher is encouraged to relate the teaching process to the student's local environment and customs; and he is given the latitude to determine how and when the students will turn from one subject to another during the school day, and how they will integrate or connect one to another—no reading or spelling period as such, for example, is set aside. Although general goals were indicated, the interest of the children was supposed to determine how the day would be divided. Here, as in the presentation of the idea of self-activity, one finds a rather explicit criticism of pre-war associationist educational psychologies, in which it had been taken for granted that everything could, and should, be broken down into "unit ideas," which meant in practice that the teaching of different subjects was rigidly compartmentalized. In the case of Wittgenstein's *Wörterbuch*, the self-activity of the students in compiling their own dictionaries, which alerted them to an awareness of the ambiguities of their own usage, was integrated with the local environment through the use of dialect.

One could cite numerous additional anecdotes and

examples to illustrate Wittgenstein's style of combining the various principles of the school-reform program. The excursions to Vienna mentioned above provide an appropriate final example. On these jaunts the children usually spent two nights in Vienna, where Mining put them up for the night at her school in Grinzing. But the integration began the moment the children assembled for departure in Trattenbach. As they hiked through the woods to catch the train from Gloggnitz, Wittgenstein required them to identify the local plants and stones, samples of which they had already studied in class. While they wandered through the streets of Vienna he threw a barrage of questions and information at them, calling their attention to machines, architectural styles, or other things they had already learned about at school. For instance, at the Technical Museum the children had to explain the models of steam engines, block-and-tackle, pulleys, and other mechanisms by reference to what they had studied in class. In Trattenbach Wittgenstein had taught his pupils the laws of the lever; now he asked them to apply those laws to specific examples. When they reached St. Stephen's Cathedral, they identified the reliefs and the different styles of architecture, such as gothic and baroque, which they had already drawn in school. As they walked through the city, or into the Palace of Schönbrunn, Wittgenstein pointed out the different kinds of columns—Corinthian, Ionian, Doric—and asked for identification. Only at the very end of the trip did the intensive questioning abate. The return train did not reach Gloggnitz until after nightfall, and the children had to make the twelve-mile hike with Wittgenstein through the dark forest. Sensing that some of them were frightened, Wittgenstein quietly went from one to another, asking: "Are you afraid? Well, then, you must think only about God." The non-Christian "Evangelist," who began and ended each school day with the Pater Noster, did not attack the religion of his villagers any more than he attacked their dialect.

## IX

In Austria as a whole, the reform in the elementary schools was often criticized by those in the upper schools and Gymnasia for emphasizing activity at the expense of content. Wittgenstein, however, achieved stunning results in mathematics, teaching ten- and eleven-year-old boys advanced algebra and geometry. About a third of his male pupils learned to handle mathematical theory and tasks that were usually not taught at all in elementary school, but introduced only in Gymnasium. He also took his students far beyond ordinary elementary-school standards in the study of history, and in literature he and his students read together not only folk and fairy tales, but also the type of poem that they would usually not encounter before the equivalent of the American junior high or high school.

One might suppose, from such an emphasis on content and achievement, that this teacher—to get his peasant students "out of the muck"—would have liked them to forsake country life. Wittgenstein did from time to time, with little success, encourage a few of his pupils to continue their studies beyond elementary school, but he did not encourage them to leave the land. Rather, it appears that he sought to awaken them to the life of the spirit, to the activity of thinking for themselves. Perhaps most of all, he tried to infuse in them a devotion to honesty. Rather than breaking them away from the village and practical tasks, he attempted to transform their attitude toward the kind of life they led, to turn them into peasants who would want their children to educate themselves.

To convey some sense of his aims, his flexibility in dealing with different students and family situations, and also to give an idea of the opposition he encountered from parents, it is worth touching briefly on his efforts with three of his best students: Emmerich Koderhold, Karl Gruber, and Oskar Fuchs.

Emmerich Koderhold, who later, after the Second World War, served for fourteen years as mayor of Trattenbach, is the prosperous farmer son of a prosperous farmer. An intelligent and warmly extroverted man, he still remembers—and can sing for hours—the student and other songs, some of them in Latin, that Wittgenstein taught his classes; and he can still recite poems from Mörike, Keller, and Schiller that Wittgenstein expected his students to memorize. His talent was obvious to Wittgenstein, who, during his second year in Trattenbach, which was Koderhold's final school year, called on Koderhold's father to tell him that his son had the ability to do advanced study, that he ought to do so, and that he was willing to help make arrangements in Vienna. His father would have none of it and explained politely to Wittgenstein that he needed a successor to carry on his farm. "Of course you do," answered Wittgenstein, "but he'll even carry the manure better if he studies."

Wittgenstein finally talked Koderhold's father into permitting his boy to visit a Gymnasium in Vienna; but Wittgenstein could not go along, Koderhold was lodged with an old woman, appears to have been lonely, and didn't get enough to eat. After a few days he returned home—to the considerable relief of his father—with no great opinion of student life in Vienna; and eventually he did take over the farm. Yet the man is clearly no ordinary peasant farmer or, to use Karl Wittgenstein's words, a "hindrance to progress." He is an educated farmer, Gymnasium education or not. He speaks High German as well as the village dialect and maintains a lively interest in world affairs as well as in Trattenbach and Austrian politics.

Karl Gruber, Wittgenstein's favorite and most talented student, impresses in a different way. He came from a poor family of six children, several of whom attended Wittgenstein's classes. Like his teacher, Karl was introverted and reflective as well as talented, and Wittgenstein became intensely fond of him. He did not object to Karl's helping less able students to do their homework in order to earn bread for himself and his brothers and sisters. A year older than the others, Karl proceeded to continue studying with Wittgenstein privately after formally finishing school in 1921. Each day, from four o'clock in the afternoon until seven in the evening, Wittgenstein conducted him through lessons in advanced Latin, Greek, and mathematics. Usually the two took dinner together in Wittgenstein's room above the grocery. Wittgenstein obviously enjoyed the boy's companionship, and throughout that year only Ludwig Hänsel's bimonthly visits to Trattenbach interrupted Karl's daily lessons. Even then the boy was not forgotten. Hänsel, who was by this time a Gymnasium professor in Vienna, acted as Karl's external examiner, quizzing him in history, geography, Latin, and other subjects that he needed to qualify for a Gymnasium in Vienna.

Eventually Wittgenstein concluded that he must adopt Karl to ensure that he did get a proper education in the capital, an education for which his parents, unlike Koderhold's, could never have paid. Karl was willing to be adopted, and Wittgenstein called on his family to propose an arrangement under which he would supervise Karl's further studies in Vienna and bear all costs. Frau Gruber was willing to entertain the proposal, but the father bluntly told Wittgenstein that further education for his son was out of the question, that he had probably already had too much, and that a boy of his age ought to be working for his own money. After Wittgenstein had left the house, the elder Gruber declared him a "crazy fellow" ("ein verrückter Kerl") to whom he could hardly entrust his son.

So Karl Gruber did go to work, and when Wittgenstein left Trattenbach for Puchberg at the end of that year his lessons ended. Yet he eventually did break away from his family and go to Vienna, unlike most of his school fellows, who remained either in Trattenbach or in one of the other villages of Neunkirchen. After finding a job for himself in Vienna, Karl tried to contact Wittgenstein, only to learn that he had left Vienna for Cambridge. He contemplated writing to him, but decided against it. In due course he married and became a post office official in Vienna. Lacking credentials, he never attained the kind of success for which his intelligence suited him, but managed nonetheless to provide an adequate and sometimes comfortable city life for himself and his family. Today he reflects wistfully that, had Wittgenstein succeeded in adopting him, he too might have become a university professor of philosophy. Any such turn of events might well have distressed Wittgenstein, who urged even some of his most talented Cambridge students to avoid professional philosophy.

Still, Wittgenstein left his mark here. Gruber impresses by his difference from Wittgenstein's other village students. Even Koderhold refers to Gruber's intelligence with reverential awe. And when Gruber returns to visit Trattenbach, his old colleagues and friends greet him with a kind of reserved respect that they do not pay to one another. Nor has he forgotten his teacher: he treasures his mementos of his school days with Wittgenstein, and he alone among Wittgenstein's old pupils was aware of the general course of Wittgenstein's career.

The third student in whom Wittgenstein took a deep interest, Oskar Fuchs, died several years ago, before this study was begun. For information on him and his relationship to Wittgenstein one has to rely chiefly on two sources: a brief but impressive manuscript account of Wittgenstein's activities in Neunkirchen prepared in 1964 by Frau Luise Hausmann, a high school English teacher in Kirchberg-am-Wechsel, and a marvelous letter from Wittgenstein to Fuchs which, one hopes, Wittgenstein's executors will one day publish. Although Fuchs, as one of Wittgenstein's brightest pupils, also received private instruction from him, Wittgenstein apparently did not encourage him to continue with formal studies. Fuchs recalled to Frau Hausmann that Wittgenstein expressed his delight when Fuchs announced that he wanted to become a shoemaker like his father. "A man has to have something ordinary to do," Wittgenstein commented, "in order to be able to let off steam." Why Wittgenstein reacted differently to Fuchs, one cannot determine. Perhaps he was less talented than the others, certainly his home life was happier, and possibly Wittgenstein, who was deeply hurt when the Gruber family rejected his overtures, may have been unwilling to chance being rejected once again. He had in any case already been rebuffed by the Fuchs family. Wittgenstein had wanted to take Fuchs to Vienna with him at Christmastime to see a play at the Burgtheater, but was evasively refused, Fuchs's mother having opposed the idea of his going off with "the weird fellow." It is also possible that Wittgenstein surmised that any attempt on his part to sponsor Fuchs would, if successful, have a crushing effect on Karl Gruber, who had keenly wanted to get away from home to study in Vienna.

In any event, Wittgenstein and Fuchs kept in touch. A year and a half after Wittgenstein's departure from Trattenbach, the two were exchanging letters between Puchberg and Trattenbach, Wittgenstein was sending Fuchs books, and Fuchs, who was studying geology in his spare time, was mailing him samples of stones found in Trattenbach.

Emmerich Koderhold, Karl Gruber and Oskar Fuchs formed the nucleus of a small band of pupils who met with Wittgenstein after school hours or in the evening when possible. The total group was not large, consisting chiefly of his brightest students and a few "whose faces he liked." These boys often remained with Wittgenstein until eight o'clock in the evening. The subject of their discussions varied. Sometimes the daily school lesson would be continued. At other times entirely new subjects would be introduced. Wittgenstein took them off to the woods to collect stones and plants, which they would label carefully. Or, after dark, Wittgenstein taught them the constellations and a bit of elementary astronomy. It was on account of these late sessions that Wittgenstein encountered the most serious resistance from the parents.

One fact about the villages shows clearly through these brief sketches: children were an important part of the local labor pool. Most families depended on hours of help from their children, around the house, in the barns, on the farm. Karl Gruber's father was by no means satisfied with the bread his son could earn helping other students do their homework; he wanted him to get a job. Emmerich Koderhold, like Oskar Fuchs, was being groomed to take over his father's business or occupation. With these economic facts of village life Wittgenstein was actively interfering; in building up his cadre of disciples, he was stealing the time—and the affection—of his pupils from their families.

Nor, despite complaints, would Wittgenstein desist from his after-hours instruction. In Puchberg and Otterthal, as in Trattenbach, he followed the same pattern with successive groups. In more prosperous Puchberg he encountered comparatively little resistance, but in Otterthal, where the children's evening work on the farms was important indeed, Wittgenstein finally faced quite fierce, active, and vicious opposition.

## X

The ground for his eventual undoing in Otterthal in 1926 had unwittingly been laid four years earlier in Trattenbach, when another of Wittgenstein's favored students, Karl Gruber's brother Konrad, had played a trick on his teacher that was to make his "practice of corporal punishment" the talk of the town. During a geography lesson Wittgenstein had once slapped Konrad for poor performance. Surreptitiously Konrad put his pencil into his nose until it bled. The sight of blood caused some commotion; Konrad was permitted to leave the room to stop the bleeding, but in fact, according to his own account some forty-five years later, he managed to extend the bleeding for the remainder of the lesson. The story about how Wittgenstein had given Konrad a bloody nose quickly spread throughout the town. By this time Konrad was too deeply involved to admit what he had done; some of the other children, however, learned what had really happened and tried similar tricks themselves. For example, when told to stand in the corner as a punishment, a pupil would stand for five minutes or so and then pretend to swoon and fall to the floor. So it came to be said in Trattenbach and Otterthal that Wittgenstein's rough discipline caused children to bleed and to faint.

What are the facts? Those of his pupils who are alive avow that Wittgenstein certainly did cane his boys when they were very naughty and that he slapped their cheeks for minor offenses. But according to these same students, Wittgenstein used his rod not one whit more than did the other teachers and differed from them only in that he used it fairly, consistently and predictably. His punishment was neither arbitrary nor whimsical, and he never took a student by surprise. Although many educators today would oppose, just as did many school reformers in Austria, any sort of corporal punishment, they usually agree that the worst possible system of rewards and punishments, whether corporal or otherwise, is one that is vacillating, where the child is left in a state of anxiety-producing uncertainty about the consequences of his actions. Wittgenstein did not vacillate: he was firm, consistent, and made thoroughly clear to his pupils what sorts of behavior would result in punishment. One sort of behavior that was *invariably* punished was dishonesty; and one way to escape punishment was to confess honestly when Wittgenstein demanded an explanation. For instance, one day in class he inquired how many pupils knew the months of the year. A number of the children raised their hands, and Wittgenstein asked each one in turn. As it happened, very few were in fact able to recite the months, whereupon Wittgenstein became very angry. Turning to Konrad Gruber, one of those who had raised his hands but had not known, Wittgenstein demanded an explanation. Konrad replied: "Because I was ashamed not to know." For his candid answer Konrad escaped punishment. The same was true of the others: those who could provide explanations for their dishonesty were spared; those who could not were punished.

A comparable episode took place at Carnival Time during Wittgenstein's second year in Trattenbach. Farmer Traht sent some doughnuts to Wittgenstein, which, as usual, were fetched by one of the pupils. On the way to Wittgenstein's room the boy ate two of the doughnuts himself. The following day in class, Wittgenstein asked him: "How many of my doughnuts did you eat?" The boy turned crimson, flabbergasted that Wittgenstein should have found out what he had done, but he replied, "I ate two of them." When Wittgenstein heard his reply, he thanked the boy for his truthfulness, did not punish him, but instead explained that Farmer Traht had enclosed a slip of paper, unnoticed by the student, with the number "13," a baker's dozen, written on it.

But Konrad Gruber, with his self-induced bloody nose, and the other children who had "fainted," had unwittingly laid the groundwork for a great lie. The man who had so captivated the children of Trattenbach and Otterthal that they would spend long hours after class with him, risking punishment for bad behavior rather than returning to their families—this man was to be formally charged with sadistic punishment of his pupils.

The crisis flared up in April 1926. According to the villagers, a genuine "conspiracy" against Wittgenstein had formed by this time. The leader, or at any rate, the chief agitator, was a man named Piribauer, who is said to have spent months "waiting in ambush" for an opportunity to "get Wittgenstein into trouble." His opportunity came at last when Wittgenstein slapped on the cheeks a child whose foster mother dwelt in Piribauer's house. The child is supposed to have been carried swooning into the school office. Those of Wittgenstein's old students who had faked fainting themselves believe today that this boy too was faking. But there is no way to know.

In any event, Piribauer and his neighbors in Otter-thal instituted legal proceedings against Wittgenstein. When they confronted him, he commented quietly, "If you intend to rise up against me, that doesn't matter to me, provided only that you are agreed among yourselves. I am ready for you," whereupon he abruptly left town, never to teach elementary school again. A trial in Glogg-nitz followed, interrupted by a compulsory psychiatric examination to determine Wittgenstein's mental respon-sibility. Wittgenstein was acquitted, but firmly refused to consider continuing to teach school. He had had enough of Tolstoy's noble serfs; and by this time even Kundt, who had cautioned Wittgenstein about the hos-tility of the Otterthalers, seems to have accepted the fact that it would be pointless for him to continue teaching in that district.

## XI

If taken strictly in isolation, these closing events in Witt-genstein's career as a schoolmaster might appear odd but, apart from their having happened to Wittgenstein, of little importance. But against the background of the school-reform program and Austrian politics, they are far more significant.

If a complaint about rough discipline was permitted to get as far as it did—namely, to force Wittgenstein to stand trial—there must have been more than a question of discipline behind it. For even allowing for Wittgen-stein's not entirely deserved reputation as a strict dis-ciplinarian, one has to remember that corporal punishment was quite common at this time. School discipline of the roughest sort had been common in the Hapsburg domains and was still widely prevalent in the twenties and thirties, although it had by that time become a subject for debate among school reformers themselves. Thus it is on the face of it unlikely that Wittgenstein's colleagues would not have supported him against a parent's complaint, even if the charge were true.

A rather more complicated explanation of the whole incident occurs. A disciplinary complaint appears to have been the pretext for a more deep-seated objection. The "conspiracy" against Wittgenstein, the details of which we are no longer likely to learn, was led by some of the villagers, like Piribauer, some of the district clerics (but not Neururer), and some of Wittgenstein's colleagues. And it was political as well as personal in nature: it came at a highly charged time throughout Austria, in the spring of 1926, when the school-reform program suffered a setback in the countryside from which it never recovered. Once the conservative farmer forces in Otterthal sensed the national strength of the movement against the school reformers, they lost no time in using the first pretext they could find to send packing back to Vienna a man who must have threatened and offended them on many levels. Wittgenstein was, despite his ascetic life, still thought to be rich; he was known to be a socialist; he was known not to be a Roman Catholic; he was a proponent of progressive education, was the author of a positivist tract, was known by the villagers to be homosexual (how, one does not know), was considered by the women of the village to be misogynistic; and, what must have been hardest to bear, he was an extremely successful teacher for all that, so much so that he had weaned the most talented children in town away from their homes.

The persecution of Wittgenstein in Otterthal was in any case no isolated incident. The compromises effected among the Austrian political parties as a result of the disturbances of 1926 meant in practice that wherever Social Democrats remained dominant, as in Vienna, Glöckel's basic program could be maintained. In the countryside, however, the Catholic party of Christian Socialists obtained firm control in most districts. After his loss of national office Glöckel became administrative president of the Vienna School Council and remained in that capacity until 1934, when the Dollfuss dictatorship, whose main support came from the country, ended school reform entirely, arrested many of its leaders, including Glöckel, and forced its chief publications, the journals *Die Quelle* and *Schulreform* (to which Wittgenstein had for a time subscribed), to cease publication. During the censorship that followed, these journals were even locked up in the National Library and were thus made inaccessible to the general reader. Educational reform was thought to be dangerous indeed.

Even Wittgenstein's friend Hänsel, who had at first been a glowingly enthusiastic supporter of the reform program, later—for political, social, and religious reasons—turned against it bitterly. Eventually he even published a polemical tract against school reform: *Der neuen Schule entgegen.*

## XII

The story just told has focused on Trattenbach and Otterthal, where Wittgenstein taught from 1920 to 1922 and 1924 to 1926 respectively. This has meant neglecting Puchberg am Schneeberg, where he taught during the two intervening years. Wittgenstein's experience there was rather different from that at the other two villages. At Puchberg he was *comparatively* happy.

Puchberg is now, and was even during the twenties, a fairly prosperous resort town. It is also larger, with a population of over three thousand, being rather more town than village. And it is lovelier by far. It brought Wittgenstein a friend—not another Neururer, a possessed crusader like himself, but a charmingly modest yet talented young music teacher, the pianist Rudolf Koder. Koder, who with his wife and family later moved to Vienna, became a lifelong friend of Wittgenstein's and a welcome guest of the family as well.

Then too, by the time Wittgenstein was settled in Puchberg the *Tractatus* had finally been published and was getting considerable philosophical attention in England. F. P. Ramsey made his pilgrimages to Wittgenstein in Puchberg. Wittgenstein also hit it off with the local priest and—despite the forebodings that he related to Russell—had more or less cordial relations with his colleagues. With one of them, the mathematics teacher Norbert Rosner, he enjoyed something approaching friendship: Wittgenstein endeavored, at Rosner's request, to reeducate him in mathematics. He did not, by Rosner's own account, appear to have had much success, but Rosner was nonetheless eager to learn, and their relations remained amicable. The school principal in Puchberg also admired Wittgenstein immensely, remarking of him: "This man is already able to do everything that I myself should like to be able to do."

*Wittgenstein with his schoolchildren in Puchberg, spring 1923.*

The tranquillity need not be overestimated. Quite the contrary, Wittgenstein behaved in Puchberg as he had in Otterthal and Trattenbach. He was strict with the children, performed educational feats with them that were as impressive, built experimental models and constructed skeletons, and treated the children of Puchberg to an excursion to Vienna.

In Puchberg too, Wittgenstein played town eccentric. Following a spat with his landlady he had to move, and this time he managed to find an unbelievably tiny room only eighteen feet square where, so it is said, he would practice his clarinet under the covers after ten o'clock at night. He practiced music with Rudolf Koder daily and took long walks with him. But when Arvid Sjögren would arrive for a visit, as he did regularly, the villagers came to attention and watched in quiet amusement. Sjögren, who was unmusical, would lie down on a bench or on the floor and fall fast asleep while Wittgenstein and Koder practiced. When Wittgenstein eventually located someone who was musical to join their sessions, he found him in the most unlikely place. A local coal miner, named Postl, joined Wittgenstein and Koder to form a musical trio. Later Wittgenstein saw to it that his family in Vienna hired Postl as a retainer, and the man spent the remainder of his working years in the service of the Stonboroughs.

The difference between Puchberg and the other villages appears to have been simple enough. The townspeople of Puchberg were more prosperous and ambitious; and they were, through their resort and tourist trade, more familiar with the ways of city folk. They valued Wittgenstein for the success he enjoyed with their children and were not so dependent economically on them. Thus Wittgenstein's after-hours sessions with his pupils in Puchberg brought only a few minor complaints. In distance, Puchberg was close to Otterthal; in time, nearer to Vienna.

## XIII

The months following Wittgenstein's departure from Otterthal marked a period of deep transition in his life. On June 3, some six weeks after his departure from Otterthal, his mother died. The remainder of that summer he spent in retreat in a monastery of the Barmherzige Brüder in Hütteldorf, a suburb of Vienna. Although Wittgenstein worked as a gardener, as he had done once before, he entertained seriously the idea of becoming a monk. The monastery no longer exists, and its buildings now serve as a home for destitute mothers and their children; yet some of the old retainers still remain, and a few remember Wittgenstein as "a very good and highly industrious gardener—and a left-winger"!

When the summer of 1926 had passed and Wittgenstein returned to Vienna, he drew closer to his family than for some years, and entered into a project for his sister Margarete Stonborough which eventually led him out of his shell and into an adult world from which he would venture back to philosophy. Margarete had undertaken to build a large mansion on a great piece of land, nearly a city block in area, in the Kundmanngasse. Once part of the grounds of the Palais Rasumofsky, the land lay directly across the street from the Teachers Training College that Wittgenstein had attended during 1919–20. Wittgenstein came to play a dominant role in the construction of the house, and is often named, together with his friend Paul Engelmann, as coarchitect.

Hitherto the role of neither man has been very clear, the less so since Engelmann himself gave most of the credit for the house to Wittgenstein. The facts are otherwise. The basic plan of the house was drawn up by Engelmann, and his original sketchbooks, corresponding closely to the final plan and drawn up at a time when Wittgenstein was still teaching school in the villages, have been preserved. In exterior appearance the house is highly derivative of the work of Engelmann's teacher, the great Viennese architect Adolf Loos, as a comparison with some of Loos's other work, such as "The Steiner House" in Vienna, which had been built as early as 1910, easily shows.[21] The most striking individual feature, the use of tall floor-to-ceiling windows in much of the house, was introduced by Margarete herself, who had used a similar device successfully some five years earlier when reconstructing her country villa at Gmunden. Wittgenstein's contribution to the house in Vienna was twofold: he introduced certain engineering features—part of the electrical system and the heating system; and he supervised the workmen in the most meticulously careful and exacting way during the construction of the building. No one who has had a house built will underestimate the importance of such work. Important as it was, however, it cannot correctly be said—as it often

[21] See Bannister Fletcher, A *History of Architecture*, 17th ed. (New York: Scribners, 1961), pp. 1072f.

is said—that Wittgenstein, in the spirit of the Renais-
sance man, not only constructed two great philosophies
but also designed one of the most original European
houses of the twentieth century. What the activity connected with the building of this house *did* do for him
was, at the very least, to draw him back more closely into
a cosmopolitan and educated society of adults. During
this period he began his meetings with Schlick, Waismann, and other members of the Vienna Circle and
began to discuss philosophy again. Thus his time as an
architect prepared him psychologically, if in no other
way, for his eventual decision to return to philosophy
and to Cambridge in January 1929. For the second time
in his life engineering paved the way to philosophy.

# 4

## THE LANGUAGE GAME

回 回 回

*One wonders what philosophy would have been like in Britain and the United States had it not been for the accident of Wittgenstein, for he might not have been on the scene at all. . . . I mean that he became known to the world of philosophy through the very special circumstances of making a strong impression on Bertrand Russell and being accepted into the world of philosophy through the bold initiative of Cambridge. Nature is wasteful, and if one wants to get something exceptionally good one must take great risks about having a great deal that is simply wild. I am sure that both Russell and Cambridge were right to adopt such a policy; and Cambridge is probably the only university in the world that would have touched Wittgenstein at any price. Had it not been for Cambridge and had it not been for Russell—and some people would hold that he made an error of judgment—almost certainly nothing more would have been heard of Wittgenstein.*

—J. O. Wisdom [1]

### I

During Wittgenstein's prewar days in Cambridge his genius and the importance of his work were undisputed. Some nine years prior to the publication of the *Tractatus*, Russell and Moore had been ecstatic in their praise of him. Russell, as he testifies in *My Philosophical Development*,[2] radically revised his own doctrines in the

[1] J. O. Wisdom, "Esotericism," *Philosophy*, October 1959, pp. 348–49.
[2] Bertrand Russell, *My Philosophical Development* (New York: Simon and Schuster, 1959).

light of Wittgenstein's criticisms, and later, after the
war had ended, wrote to Wittgenstein's mother that he
expected the next great advance in philosophy to come
from her son. Prior to 1922, many of the best minds of
England were prepared to go to great lengths to put
Wittgenstein in the best circumstances to continue his
philosophical development. Thus Keynes's intervention
to secure Wittgenstein's release from prison-camp in
Monte Cassino (which, once secured, Wittgenstein refused), Russell's visits to The Hague and to Innsbruck
for talks with him, and the pilgrimages of Ramsey and
other young English students to Puchberg.

During the twenties there was an occasional hint
that things were not the same between Wittgenstein and
his old teachers. Russell and Wittgenstein, for example,
both departed from their meeting in Innsbruck in 1922
irritated and disgusted with one another. But not before
Wittgenstein's return to Cambridge in January 1929 did
the full extent of the change, both in Wittgenstein's way
of thinking and in his relationships with his former
teachers, begin to surface. The initial encounters, in
particular that with Moore, whom he had not seen since
April 1914 when Moore had visited him in Norway, were
largely satisfactory. It was found that Wittgenstein's
prewar residence in Cambridge could be credited toward
the Ph.D., and Wittgenstein presented the *Tractatus*
as his dissertation, with Ramsey named as his super-
visor and Moore as examiner. Owing to Ramsey's illness
and early death, Moore and Russell came to act as oral
examiners. The whimsically cordial mood of that meeting in June of 1929 is conveyed in the report that

Moore is said to have written about Wittgenstein's "thesis":

It is my personal opinion that Mr. Wittgenstein's thesis is a work of genius; but, be that as it may, it is certainly well up to the standard required for the Cambridge degree of Doctor of Philosophy.

As it turned out, the next great change in philosophy *did* stem largely from Wittgenstein's influence. But it was not the influence of the *Tractatus*, but of the "new" or "later" Wittgenstein that accounted for this. Nor was that change anything like what Russell had anticipated. Writing of Wittgenstein's "treachery to his own greatness," Russell recorded: "I admired Wittgenstein's *Tractatus* but not his later work, which seemed to me to involve an abnegation of his own best talent. . . . Its positive doctrines seem to me trivial and its negative doctrines unfounded. I have not found in Wittgenstein's *Philosophical Investigations* anything that seemed to me interesting and I do not understand why a whole school finds important wisdom in its pages." [3]

Even more vitriolic than Russell was C. D. Broad, the Knightbridge Professor of Moral Philosophy, himself a highly distinguished philosopher of science, who later, in his own intellectual autobiography, reported:

The one duty which I wittingly neglected was to attend the weekly meetings of the Moral Sciences Club. . . . I was not prepared to spend hours every week in a thick atmosphere of cigarette-smoke, while Wittgenstein punctually

[3] *Ibid.*, pp. 214–16.

went through his hoops, and the faithful as punctually "wondered with a foolish face of praise." [4]

The Cambridge authorities did not, despite rumblings of disapproval, fail to support Wittgenstein. In June of 1929 the Council of Trinity College awarded him a research grant; and on October 16 of that year, the University Faculty Board of Moral Sciences invited him to give a course of lectures. By December 1930 Wittgenstein had been elected a Research Fellow of Trinity College. The growing reserve about his work, however, perhaps best expressed itself in the exchange between Moore and Russell concerning Wittgenstein's appointment to the Trinity Fellowship.

In early March of 1930 Moore wrote to Russell, on behalf of the Council of Trinity College, asking him to prepare a report on the research Wittgenstein had been doing during the course of that academic year and to meet with Wittgenstein to discuss it. "There seems," Moore wrote, "no other way of ensuring him [Wittgenstein] a sufficient income to continue his work, unless the Council do make him a grant; and I am afraid there is very little chance that they will do so, unless they can get favourable reports from experts in the subject." Russell replied cautiously to the effect that although he did not see how he could refuse to report on Wittgenstein's work, it would involve a great deal of time; later, after a weekend discussion with Wittgenstein, Russell wrote again to Moore to ask for a delay of a month or so in making his report, "since my impressions at the mo-

[4] *The Philosophy of C. D. Broad*, ed. P. A. Schilpp (New York: Tudor Publishing Company, 1959), p. 61.

ment are rather vague, and he intends while in Austria to make a synopsis of his work which would make it much easier for me to report adequately." After a further session with Wittgenstein at the beginning of May and a study of his manuscript, Russell reported to Moore, "His theories are certainly important and certainly very original. Whether they are true, I do not know; I devoutly hope they are not, as they make mathematics and logic almost incredibly difficult. . . . I am quite sure that Wittgenstein ought to be given an opportunity to pursue his work." Two days later Moore wrote back that Russell's report as it stood would not do, and requested a more formal report for the Council's permanent records, in which Russell should emphasize his high opinion of the importance of Wittgenstein's *new* work. Russell reluctantly complied, and Wittgenstein was in due course elected a Fellow of Trinity. One need not read between the lines of this correspondence to observe that not only Russell but also the Council of Trinity College were unconvinced of the real merit of Wittgenstein's latest work.[5]

## II

This doubt lingers on in many minds today, some forty years after Wittgenstein set down the *Philosophische Bemerkungen* (the work that Russell read for Trinity College) and the *Philosophische Grammatik*, the first

[5] The correspondence in question, together with Russell's formal report to Trinity College, is printed in *The Autobiography of Bertrand Russell*, Vol. II.

works written more or less in the manner of his later philosophy. Although Wittgenstein's work was for many years more influential in the English-speaking countries than that of any other philosopher, it was also the most sharply criticized.

While some quite obscure passages appear in the *Tractatus*, it was nonetheless a systematic work the gist of whose aims and content might be summarized. With almost all of Wittgenstein's later work, even *Philosophical Investigations*, the most finished statement of his later ideas, the situation is otherwise. The intent and aim of the work, other than the part that is purely polemical, are less than clear; and the work is written in a style that hardly lends itself to summary form, since some of the chief points are exhibited or insinuated rather than being stated. The difficulty in coming to grips with this later work explains the existence of such a large secondary literature of books, articles, and anthologies devoted to its clarification and explanation as well as to its criticism. In preparing this essay, I read much of this secondary literature while rereading Wittgenstein's own work. My experience was, so I understand, similar to that of many others: I was often unable to locate in his own writings theses widely attributed to him by commentators. A connected problem is that the commentaries contain widely varying interpretations of his later thought, as well as widely varying conceptions of where its emphasis falls and its importance lies.

Thus I begin my account of Wittgenstein's later work with a reminder of the difference between his own philosophy, itself highly controversial, and any number of positions, differing to a greater or lesser extent, which may be dubbed part of "*Wittgensteinian* philosophy," in that they emphasize the influence of Wittgenstein's work on their work; address themselves to problems, formulations, and examples drawn from his work; and are frequently composed by philosophers who either studied with Wittgenstein or else were in close contact with those who did, whether as students or colleagues.

To write about Wittgensteinian philosophy would be to undertake to write a history of a large portion of a philosophical era in Britain and North America, dating at least since the early thirties, when Wittgenstein's later ideas began to be disseminated through his teaching at Cambridge and reports of this teaching by way of lecture notes and books and articles inspired by him. This essay has no such aim: I aspire to do no more than give a brief report of his own work.

## III

The earliest expression of Wittgenstein's later views is usually dated in the late twenties. Some of the changes in his outlook emerged during his conversations with Schlick and Waismann in 1928, and Wittgenstein himself reports that his conversations with Ramsey and Piero Sraffa in Cambridge in 1929 forced a radical change in his thinking. From 1929 to 1933 he recorded in two large manuscripts, now published posthumously in German as *Philosophische Bemerkungen* and *Philosophische Grammatik*, some of the main shifts in his position. By the early 1930s, if the Notes of Wittgen-

stein's lectures which Moore published after Wittgenstein's death are accurate, many of the leitmotivs of his
later work and the details of his rejection of his earlier
work had already been displayed. These received a more
polished preliminary statement in English in *The Blue
Book* and *The Brown Book*, two typescripts named after
the colors of the covers in which they were bound,
which Wittgenstein dictated during 1933–35, and which
are direct forerunners of *Philosophical Investigations*.
Several other works have also been published posthumously. Never intended for publication by Wittgenstein,
these works, such as *Zettel* and *Remarks on the Foundations of Mathematics*, have been collated by his executors in the form of remarks. These unfinished, and sometimes very rough, treatments of various problems are
nonetheless useful in illustrating Wittgenstein's application of his new method of philosophizing to a wide
range of examples.

Just how and precisely when Wittgenstein changed
his philosophical approach provides a historical puzzle
that probably cannot be solved. It is quite possible that
he himself did not become aware of the extent to which
his philosophical outlook had shifted until the late
twenties. But there is evidence that the change began
earlier, long before his contact with the members of the
Vienna Circle and his return to Cambridge. I have
already mentioned the anecdote that Wittgenstein told
his student in Trattenbach in 1921 about an experiment
aimed to determine whether three persons who had
learned no language would, if shut away from the world,
learn or invent a primitive language for themselves,
an anecdote whose themes anticipate some of his later

concerns with private languages and with the conditions of language acquisition.

This example, as well as the character of some of Wittgenstein's earliest conversations with Schlick and Waismann, suggests that he had already departed from the *Tractatus* by the late twenties and, moreover, had a fairly definite idea of what was wrong with it and in what direction a more satisfactory way of philosophizing would lead. What triggered the change? There are of course *legends* about the metamorphosis; for example, Wittgenstein is said to have attributed the change to his realization that he could not "analyze" a Neapolitan gesture made by Sraffa. But even if the anecdote is genuine, it explains the change in Wittgenstein's outlook about as much—and as little—as the story about the apple explains Newton's theory of gravitation.

My own conjecture is that the themes of the Austrian school-reform movement, which were deeply opposed to Wittgenstein's early work, gradually—and perhaps quite contrary to his intentions or expectations—eroded his earlier beliefs and insinuated themselves in their place. If any individual thinker can be said to have influenced Wittgenstein during the course of this change, it must have been Karl Bühler (1879–1963), Professor of Philosophy at the University of Vienna and at the Vienna Pedagogical Institute and chief theoretician of the school-reform movement.[6]

[6] Since I arrived at my conclusion that Bühler and Wittgenstein must have been connected, several other scholars have reached similar conclusions. See, for example: Stephen Toulmin, "Ludwig Wittgenstein," *Encounter* 1969, and "Ludwig Wittgenstein, Karl Bühler and Psycholinguistics," mimeographed, 1968. See also Bernard Kaplan, "Comments on S. Toulmin's 'Wittgenstein, Bühler and the Psychology of Language,'" mim-

## IV

An implicit child psychology had undergirded Glöckel's reforms; to wit, a theory of the child as an active social being whose mind was far more than an empty bucket to be filled with appropriate information. In their attack on the Drillschule and Lernschule, the reformers were quite explicitly anti-Herbartian, antiassociationist, and antiatomist in learning theory and psychology. The alternative learning theory and educational philosophy that were taught at the University of Vienna, the Pedagogical Institute in Vienna, and the various teacher training colleges were dominated by the views of Bühler, who—together with his wife Charlotte, herself an eminent child psychologist—had been lured to Vienna in 1922 by Glöckel and his colleagues.[7] In 1923, only a few months after the Bühlers arrived in Vienna, Glöckel declared formally what had long been assumed: "The entire School Reform is, essentially, built on the results of psychological research into the mind of the child."[8]

eographed, 1969. The mimeographed essays by Kaplan and Toulmin, as well as an earlier treatment of this subject by myself, are forthcoming in *The Boston Studies in the Philosophy of Science*. Doctoral students at a number of American universities are at present preparing theses on the connections between Bühler and Wittgenstein, so further information on this subject may be expected in the not too distant future.

[7] For an account of Bühler's life and a complete bibliography see *Karl Bühler: Die Uhren der Lebewesen und Fragmente aus dem Nachlass*, ed. Gustav Lebzeltern (Vienna: Hermann Böhlaus Nachf., Kommissionsverlag der Österreichischen Akademie der Wissenschaften, 1969).

[8] Otto Glöckel, *Die Österreichische Schulreform* (Vienna: Verlag der Wiener Volksbuchhandlung, 1923), p. 11.

Bühler's work, particularly his *Geistige Entwicklung des Kindes* (1918), an abridged version of which later appeared in English as *The Mental Development of the Child* (1930), influenced the school-reform movement from the outset and was introduced almost at once as a textbook in pedagogy in the new teacher training colleges.

Bühlerian child psychology is a critical version of Gestalt psychology, difficult to classify precisely but perhaps closer to the thought of the Swiss psychologist Jean Piaget, whom Bühler greatly influenced, than to that of the well-known leaders of the Gestalt school: Max Wertheimer, Kurt Koffka, Wolfgang Köhler, Kurt Lewin.

Bühler himself began his career in Würzburg, Germany, where in 1906 he became assistant to Oswald Külpe, the critical realist famed for his attacks on Ernst Mach's positivism. Building on Külpe's work, Bühler began to develop a theory called "imageless thought," and extended and refined his views as he moved from Würzburg, along with Külpe, first to Bonn and then to Munich. The idea of imageless thought, as presented by Külpe and Bühler, stressed that in the intentional act of representing, the particular image or model used, if any, need bear no "imaginal" resemblance to that which it represented. Abstract words, it was claimed, are used conventionally, and neither can be, nor need be, reduced to atoms or elements, including sense impressions. Such a view was, like those put forward by the Gestalt psychologists, radically opposed to positivism and to any number of related philosophical and psychological doctrines, whether they be called associationism, reductionism, behaviorism, or logical atomism.

Like the Gestaltists, Bühler sought to show that theory making—organization—was a basic function of the human mind independent of associations of sense impressions or other "atoms of thought." The organizing and theorizing activity of the mind enjoyed a kind of priority which determined the kinds of wholes with which one would deal as "elements" in thinking. Like Köhler, whose work is better known in the English-speaking countries, Bühler insisted that his arguments against psychological atomism also defeat epistemological and philosophical atomism.

By the end of the war, Bühler had made important contributions to the theory of language and to child psychology. These subjects dominate the discussion of his *Geistige Entwicklung* and of three other important works that he published after his move to Vienna: *Die Krise der Psychologie* (1926), *Ausdruckstheorie* (1933), and *Sprachtheorie* (1934). Within Austria, and particularly in Vienna, it would be hard to overestimate the extent of his influence, nor was it confined to the Austrian Republic. As Robert Dottrens, of the Institut Jean-Jacques Rousseau in Geneva, reported:

At the conclusion of a tour through Czecho-Slovakia, Germany, Belgium, England and France, I do not hesitate to say that Vienna is ahead of all the other cities of Europe from the point of view of educational progress. . . . It is to Vienna, the pedagogical Mecca . . . that the new pilgrims of the modern school must go to find the realization of their dreams and hopes.[9]

[9] Robert Dottrens, *The New Education in Austria* (New York: The John Day Co., 1930), pp. ix and 202. Similar testimony may be found in Richard Meister, "Teacher Training in Austria," *Harvard Educational Review*, vol. 8, January 1938, pp. 112–21.

During his sixteen years in Vienna, Bühler attracted many such pilgrims—students and associates who later attained distinction in their own right, among them Paul Lazarsfeld, Egon Brunswik, Else Frenkel-Brunswik, Konrad Lorenz, Karl Popper, Lotte Schenk-Danzinger, Albert Wellek, Edward Tolman. Although his name appears in no list of Bühler's students, it appears that among the most eminent of those who learned from Bühler was Wittgenstein.

## V

Wittgenstein undoubtedly read, and was impressed by, the writings of the Gestalt psychologists. Several examples in *Philosophical Investigations* are taken from the work of Koffka, and Wittgenstein attributes his famous "duck-rabbit" example (a figure that can be seen as a duck or as a rabbit) to Jastrow—although in fact it had been part of the parlor magician's repertoire for several hundred years. Wittgenstein does not mention Bühler by name; he had taken an intense personal dislike to the man's "self-important professorial manners." Karl and Charlotte Bühler had, nonetheless, been present at the well-known first encounter between Wittgenstein and Moritz Schlick, as the guests of Wittgenstein's sister Margarete Stonborough; [10] they had been invited at the suggestion of Wittgenstein's nephew, who was studying with Bühler at the University of Vienna. From time to

[10] See Paul Engelmann, *op. cit.*, p. 118; and B. F. McGuinness in *Friedrich Waismann: Wittgenstein und der Wiener Kreis* (Oxford: Basil Blackwell, 1967), p. 15n.

time Wittgenstein would denounce Bühler as a charlatan. This personal reaction, however, far from precluding some positive intellectual influence, indicates that Wittgenstein took much more than passing interest in the man.

In the passage from *Zettel* (412) quoted earlier, Wittgenstein asks himself whether what he is doing is child psychology. *Zettel, The Blue and Brown Books,* and *Philosophical Investigations* must be read in a number of different ways; but two necessary ways are as polemics against the atomism represented by the *Tractatus* or by Russell or Herbart and as attempts to develop the outlines of a child psychology of language. How, after all, does the *Investigations* open except as a critique of Saint Augustine's account of how a child learns a language? Much of the first part of the *Investigations* focuses on the question of how children learn their native tongues.

References to Bühler and other Gestalt psychologists, therefore, crop up from time to time in my discussion of Wittgenstein's later philosophy, for there are, indeed, striking similarities between some of Bühler's leading ideas and those of the later Wittgenstein. Among these are: (1) their opposition to psychological and logical atomism; (2) in the place of atomism, a contextualism or configurationism; (3) a radical linguistic conventionalism built up in opposition to essentialist doctrines; (4) the idea of "imageless thought."

To suggest that Bühler influenced Wittgenstein is in no way to belittle Wittgenstein's own contribution. Quite the contrary, the stress on Wittgenstein's originality can be stoutly maintained. What I do wish is to shift the very English context in which Wittgenstein is usually read and to bring another, less familiar background of his thought to light. Nor do I suggest that the views of Wittgenstein and Bühler are identical. But one needs comparable theories at one's disposal before the important job of differentiation can be carried out. Both Wittgenstein and the Gestalt psychologists would have to agree that not only are shapes or figures similar or different depending on their ground or context, but *people and their ideas are also similar or different in relationship to a background.* When the missing background of the "very different" philosophies of Wittgenstein and the Gestaltists is provided, their similarities on basic issues emerge.

## VI

The *Tractatus* had recognized only one meaningful function of language: that of picturing the world. If this function was not always apparent in ordinary usage, it could nonetheless be exhibited through logical analysis of the complex into its simple atoms.

The philosophy that Wittgenstein was advocating by 1930, shortly after his return to Cambridge, differs so markedly from his earlier work that it appears that the undermining of his earlier work, begun during his school-teaching career and furthered by his exposure to Bühler and the Gestalt psychologists, was by then far advanced. Yet the development of his "later thought" continued until the very end of his life. Never did it reach the systematic shape of the *Tractatus,* and Wittgenstein

*Wittgenstein in the thirties, after his return to Cambridge.*

confessed his deep dissatisfaction with the result. In his *Philosophical Investigations* (1953), published two years after his death, he records these misgivings, comparing his new work to an "album" of philosophical remarks. These remarks could, he noted, be seen rightly "only by contrast with and against the background of" his old way of thinking as expressed in the *Tractatus*, a book that, he now declared, contained "grave mistakes" (P.I., page x).

The *Investigations* is, thus, in part a polemical attack on the ideas of his younger self. But it also develops new arguments concerning logic, meaning, thinking and understanding, language, the nature of philosophy, intended both to replace and to supplement those displaced by his criticism of the doctrines of the *Tractatus*.

That Wittgenstein should eventually have come to reject logical atomism is hardly surprising. A battery of arguments against atomism had been developed during the nineteenth century, following Kant, by both philosophers and psychologists. Although some were new, many were ancient, the novelty being the systematizing of a quite powerful war machine against atomism or, as it was often called, "elementarism." What is striking about Wittgenstein's rejection of atomism is that he rarely relied on arguments taken from this readily available canon, but developed and deployed different ones. The question is what these new arguments are, and whether they are as effective as the old, let alone superior to them.

Just as traditional atomism had tended to maintain that legitimate theory must be derivable from sense observation reports, so traditional arguments against atomism had maintained that sense observation reports untainted by theory were impossible; i.e., that all observation was theory impregnated. Moreover, these arguments continued, even if pure observation reports could, *per impossibile*, exist, these would not be sufficient to generate all legitimate theory.

In his notes on Wittgenstein's lectures, Moore reports that very soon after they began, Wittgenstein announced that his opinions had changed most with respect to elementary propositions. After pointing out that he had produced no examples of elementary propositions in the *Tractatus*, he commented that it was indeed senseless to talk of a final analysis into elementary propositions. From Moore's report alone, one might conclude that Wittgenstein was headed in the direction of a traditional critique of atomism that would show that no examples of atomic propositions had been produced because in fact no such propositions were, either psychologically or logically, possible.

It soon became evident, however, that Wittgenstein's assault on atomism was to be quite unconventional. In *The Blue and Brown Books*, as well as in *Philosophical Investigations*, he did not concern himself much with the impossibility or insufficiency of atomic propositions; rather, his argument is that they are *not needed for meaningful communication*. Yet it is not clear that many philosophers had ever claimed that meaningful communication alone required analysis into atomic propositions, or even the possibility of such analysis. The need stressed by earlier proponents of atomism had been that of sorting out legitimate from illegitimate claims. To answer this need, one resorted, when in doubt, to analysis. Earlier proponents of atomism might well have conceded, had they been asked, that analysis was not ordinarily needed for meaningful communication and that for the sort of meaning required for meaningful communication an analysis of *usage* would usually suffice.

Nonetheless, Wittgenstein's attack appears to be quite definite about its aims and assumptions. He notes that in the *Tractatus* (e.g., 3.251) he had assumed that every proposition has a perfectly determinate or definite sense, and he rehearses the reasoning that led him to that conclusion as follows:

We are under the illusion that what is peculiar, profound, essential, in our investigation, resides in its trying to grasp the incomparable essence of language. . . . The sense of a sentence—one would like to say—may, of course, leave this or that open, but the sentence must nevertheless have *a* definite sense. An indefinite sense—that would really not be a sense *at all*.—This is like: An indefinite boundary is not really a boundary at all. Here one thinks perhaps: if I say "I have locked the man up fast in the room—there is only one door left open"—then I simply haven't locked him in at all; his being locked in is a sham. One would be inclined to say here: "You haven't done anything at all." An enclosure with a hole in it is as good as *none*.—But is that true? (P.I., pars. 97–99.)

Wittgenstein answers his question firmly in the negative, rejecting the view, which he traces to Frege, that a "blurred concept" is no concept at all. "Frege," Wittgenstein remarks, "compares a concept to an area and says that an area with vague boundaries cannot be called an area at all. This presumably means that we cannot do anything with it.—But is it senseless to say: 'Stand roughly there'?" (P.I., par. 71).

The bulk of the examples Wittgenstein marshaled against the view that a sentence must have a definite sense are of the sort cited. He argued, with such homely examples, that the degree of precision required in particular cases is relative to the context and that one does not necessarily improve one's communication by heightening the degree of precision, or the extent of analysis, of a proposition.

In the course of attacking, by means of examples taken from ordinary discourse, the *a priori* requirement that each proposition have a definite sense, he comes to stress the importance in philosophy of detailed examination of ordinary language. It turns out that in language, as used, many propositions are vague, inexact, indefinite, but nonetheless quite adequately serve our purposes without demanding further analysis. His broomstick argument provides a justly famous example of the style as well as content and method of his later work:

When I say: "My broom is in the corner,"—is this really a statement about the broomstick and the brush? Well, it could at any rate be replaced by a statement giving the position of the stick and the position of the brush. And this statement is surely a further analysed form of the first one. —But why do I call it "further analysed"?—Well, if the broom is there, that surely means that the stick and brush must be there, and in a particular relation to one another; and this was as it were hidden in the sense of the first sentence, and is *expressed* in the analysed sentence. Then does someone who says that the broom is in the corner really mean: the broomstick is there, and so is the brush, and the broomstick is fixed in the brush?—If we were to ask anyone if he meant this he would probably say that he had not thought specially of the broomstick or specially of the brush at all. And that would be the *right* answer, for he meant to speak neither of the stick nor of the brush in particular. Suppose that, instead of saying "Bring me the broom," you said "Bring me the broomstick and the brush which is fitted on to it."!—Isn't the answer: "Do you want the broom? Why do you put it so oddly?"—Is he going to understand the further analysed sentence better?—This sentence, one might say, achieves the same as the ordinary one, but in a more roundabout way. [P.I., par. 60]

As an alternative to the idea that one must be able to give an exact definition or analysis of one's terms, Wittgenstein advances the notion of "family resemblances." Instead of producing something common or essential, he remarks, he wants to show that the phenomena he is discussing have no single thing in common which makes one use the same word for all, but are, rather, *related* to one another in a variety of different ways. To explain his meaning, he invites his readers to consider *games*:

I mean board-games, card-games, ball-games, Olympic games, and so on. What is common to them all?—Don't say: "There *must* be something common, or they would not be called 'games,'"—but *look and see* whether there is anything common to all.—For if you look at them you will not see something that is common to *all*, but similarities, relationships, and a whole series of them at that. To repeat: don't think, but look! Look for example at board-games, with their multifarious relationships. Now pass to card-games; here you find many correspondences with the first group, but many common features drop out, and others appear. When we pass next to ball-games, much that is common is retained, but much is lost.—Are they all "amusing"? Compare chess with noughts and crosses. Or is there always winning and losing, or competition between players? Think of patience [solitaire]. In ball games there is winning and losing; but when a child throws his ball at the wall and catches it again, this feature has disappeared. . . . And we can go through the many, many other groups of games in the same way; can see how similarities crop up and disappear.

And the result of this examination is: we see a complicated network of similarities overlapping and criss-crossing: sometimes overall similarities, sometimes similarities of detail.

I can think of no better expression to characterize these similarities than "family resemblances"; for the various resemblances between members of a family: build, features, colour of eyes, gait, temperament, etc. etc. overlap and criss-cross in the same way.—And I shall say: "games" form a family. [P.I., pars. 66–67]

The example is delightful, just as the idea of family resemblances is ingeniously applied as an alternative to essentialist-oriented analysis. Yet, unless it can be shown that atomism depended greatly on the claim that *meaningful communication* requires analysis into atomic propositions, Wittgenstein's entire discussion of essentialism and attack on analysis, even if correct both in theme and in detail, is beside the point. It was this combination of brilliance and apparent irrelevance that so angered Russell and Broad.

It might also be wondered if Wittgenstein's arguments against the philosophical program of defining —or analyzing—terms are indeed correct. To decide this issue, it is not necessary to quarrel with his claim that one may very often, and probably usually, communicate with vague and inexact language. Nor need one challenge his suggestion that to push the demand for exactness too far—to become *over*exact—is to run the risk of being silly. Nor need it be questioned whether his individual arguments showing the impossibility of giving a precise definition to certain terms such as "game" and "family resemblance" are sound. One may agree with him on all these points without granting that the necessary and sufficient conditions required in definitions can never be given—or that they are never needed. In fact, there do appear to be important cases where necessary and sufficient conditions, unique defining criteria, both can, and need to be, given. One example quite appropriate to Wittgenstein's discussion is that of *family relationships*. One may give exact definitions of words like "sibling," "mother," "father," "aunt," "guardian." And one may need to do so—in legal disputes, for instance. There are, then, some *contexts* where definitions and essences are quite in order.

This point leads to another of Wittgenstein's main arguments against atomism: the contextualism or configurationism of his later philosophy. In the *Investigations* he argues that it is senseless to talk of a one-to-one correspondence between the simples of language and those of reality (even assuming that either sort of simple existed). He reasons that simplicity is not a matter of absolutes, but is context-dependent: one might, he notes, break down the visual image of a flower into all the different colors of which it is composed—although even that, as he failed to remark, would presuppose a highly sophisticated theory of color absolutes. Even were this possible, the question of which properties are more simple, he reasons, makes little sense. Multicoloredness is one kind of complexity; being composed of straight lines is another. Since, on Wittgenstein's view, we use the

words "composite" and "simple" in a great many different ways, and ways that are also differently related,
questions that presuppose *absolute* complexity and simplicity *apart from context* are not answerable and ought
not to be asked. On this point Wittgenstein's line of
reasoning is, again, quite close to that of Bühler and the
Gestalt psychologists. Külpe, for instance, had contrived
a famous experiment with cards (which resembles Wittgenstein's example of colored boxes in *Investigations*
48) in order to combat Mach's claim that mental proc-
esses could be reduced to sensations. Külpe presented his
subjects with cards containing nonsense syllables of
various colors and arrangements. Some subjects were
asked to report on the *color*, others on the *pattern*, others
on the numbers of the items seen. In every case, the
subject abstracted those features that he had been in-
structed to report and made no mention of—and in many
cases could not remember—other features of the card
that could easily well have been taken as simples. Here
again the answers depended on the question asked, on
the context. Whereas for the associationist, organization
or theory arises from previous association, for Külpe,
Bühler and other Gestaltists—and for Wittgenstein in his
later work—association depends on organization or
theory.

## VII

In the *Tractatus* Wittgenstein had marked off legitimate scientific propositions from all other utterances.
Even if he paid little honor to scientific propositions,

which leave "the problems of life . . . completely untouched" (*Tractatus* 6.52) and show "how little is achieved" (*Tractatus*, page 5), they had pride of place in his philosophy. So when he discovered that the position of the *Tractatus* was impossible, he made a quite radical *volte face*. In the *Investigations* there is no longer any prideful place: scientific propositions connect with many other kinds, with many other language-games, no one of which enjoys the power of judging or criticizing any other, and each of which gains its meaning from the use to which it is put within some established area of discourse. If science was not authoritative, nothing was authoritative; if no atomic scientific propositions mirrored the world, then the world was not mirrored by language at all. From his discovery that *his* theory of criticism, as developed in the *Tractatus*, could not work, Wittgenstein concluded that any philosophical theory of criticism was impossible. To criticize, to justify, to explain, these were no longer proper philosophical aims: all that remained to the philosopher was to *describe* the many different sorts of language-games and the "forms of life" in which they were embedded. Such description was in itself *subject-neutral*: while attempting to bring out—to describe—the logics or grammars of various kinds of discourse, it could not *in principle* presume to elevate one of these above another. Even the basic laws of logic, which logicians were having some measure of success at articulating, were now to be regarded as *conventions*, as highly systematic schemes for ordering statements which, far from "making manifest" the logical structure of the world, were man-created schemes of classification, *in no way more basic* than other language-games, which were also man-created. A sophisticated anthropocentric relativism, a kind of comparative anthropology of linguistic systems whose meaning was determined by their usage, replaced the objective realism of the *Tractatus*.

One thing, however, had evidently not changed; namely, Wittgenstein's conviction that the solution of the *Tractatus* was "definitive and unassailable": it had stated how analysis into simples would *have to* proceed if there was to be any such analysis. If *his* account did not work, *no* such account could work!

Wittgenstein's later radical subjectivism is—despite occasional claims to the contrary—no more Kantian than was his earlier realism. Nonetheless, there are in the later Wittgenstein echoes of some Kantian themes: to the extent that the categories, logics, grammars, frameworks of different language-games are seen as records of the natural history of man's interaction with his environment, rather than as reflections of the structure of the world, there is a *touch* of Kantianism there. Human language, embedded in human conduct, is taken as the starting point for an investigation which no longer assumes that the exploration of human language gives access to reality, but rather proposes that human language, as a *projection* of the mind rather than a picture of the world, in a sense *creates* reality. Yet here too the differences with Kant are basic. For Kant the structure of the world was unknowable and the categories of the understanding unchanging; for the early Wittgenstein the structure of the world was knowable; for the later Wittgenstein the categories of the understanding—of language—were in constant flux.

## VIII

In the *Philosophical Investigations*, then, the claim that one single language of science exists is dropped and introduced in its stead is the view that language consists of a multitude of different, often interacting, language-games, each with its own "grammar" or rules of use. The word "grammar," as used here and by Wittgenstein, does not refer to the school grammar of subject and predicate, noun, verb, adjective and other "parts of speech," a system of classification which Wittgenstein viewed as highly misleading. Very likely he chose quite deliberately to use this old word in a new way, for just as school grammar was tied closely to the theory of Aristotelian logic, rendered obsolete by the work of Frege, Russell and Whitehead, Wittgenstein and others, just so was his new sense of grammar as "depth grammar" or "the underlying logic of a language" linked to the new logic. In fact, Wittgenstein uses the word "grammar" in at least two senses, neither of which corresponds to school grammar. The first, surface grammar, concerns the way in which a word is used in the construction of a particular utterance; the second, depth grammar, relies more on the *point* of the language-game or form of life in which that word plays some part.[11]

[11] Wittgenstein's depth grammar does not, contrary to what is occasionally suggested, correspond to Chomsky's deep grammar, as expounded in his linguistic theory.

## IX

It is not necessary for the later Wittgenstein that all, or even any, of the languages that concern the philosopher have the particular grammar of being reducible to atomic propositions, nor is philosophical bewilderment or puzzlement any longer attributed to the use of utterances that are not analyzable into atomic propositions.

His concern, however, is still to eliminate philosophical puzzlement, and his whole view of the nature of philosophy hinges on his understanding of this concern. His program for eliminating philosophy, a program that he regarded as "a battle against the bewitchment of our intelligence by means of language" (P.I. 109), depends on the explanation he provides for the *origin* of this puzzlement. In the *Philosophical Investigations* philosophical perplexity is traced to several main sources of error. One is to be "held captive" by a picture—of time, say, as a stream. A second is to confuse surface and depth grammar. A more important error is a third: becoming confused about the complex interaction of different language-games, applying the rules of one language-game erroneously to another, mixing different grammars. When this occurs, an important utterance may quite inadvertently be jerked out of its proper context. "A wheel that can be turned though nothing else moves with it, is not part of the mechanism" (P.I. 271).

The sort of error that Wittgenstein sees as the source of philosophical perplexity is very much like that often described by contemporary analytic philosophers as a "category mistake," although Wittgenstein himself does not use this terminology.[12] To avoid category mistakes it becomes necessary to undertake the detailed study of ordinary language, the study of language in context in all its interactions with life, behavior, nature. Wittgenstein writes (P.I. 7): "I shall also call the whole, consisting of language and the actions into which it is woven, the 'language-game.' "

Through detailed "purely descriptive" studies of "what has to be accepted, the given . . . ," Wittgenstein tries to explain how one learns the "proper use" within a socially fixed "language-game" or form of life of various expressions; in learning this proper use, one learns the rules of the game in which the expressions occur. Language will then trespass its limits, or "go on holiday" as he puts it, when particular sorts of expressions are used outside their proper domain or range of application. Thus philosophical critique becomes the activity of showing how language may stray from its proper place and then bringing it back to its correct context.

The *Tractatus*, taken as a whole, is thus regarded as itself one grand category-mistake, in this case that of supposing that different language-games must satisfy the criteria of one supremely authoritative language-game— namely, science. Wittgenstein presents in the *Investigations*, and in other later writings, numerous examples

[12] But compare Friedrich Waismann's semiofficial exposition of Wittgenstein's later thought in *The Principles of Linguistic Philosophy* (London: Macmillan, 1965), p. 104.

of such "grammatical" errors. Many of these have to do with what he regards as our tendency to impose on our *mental* concepts tasks and rules appropriate at best to our physical concepts, and often not even to them. A tendency to mix mental with physical concepts goes far, he suggests, to explain why philosophers spend so much time arguing about the existence of "Mental Substance" and dividing themselves into Monists and Dualists. These old disagreements, Wittgenstein suggests, are not disagreements about matters of fact, as they appeared to be to most of those who engaged in them, but are, rather, rooted in such mistakes as misapplying the grammar of mental concepts to the grammar of physical concepts and vice versa, and taking words out of their proper grammatical context.

Wittgenstein is led by this route to devote a large part of the *Investigations* to mental concepts, to the study of words such as "thinking," "feeling," "meaning," "understanding," "intending." Here he develops an idea of "imageless thought" closely resembling that of Külpe and Bühler. "There is a lack of clarity," he writes,

about the role of imaginability in our investigation. Namely, about the extent to which it insures that a proposition makes sense. It is no more essential to the understanding of a proposition that one should imagine anything in connexion with it, than that one should make a sketch from it. Instead of "imaginability" one can also say here: representability by a particular method of representation. And such a representation may indeed safely point a way to further use of a sentence. On the other hand a picture may obtrude itself upon us and be of no use at all. [P.I. 395, 396, 397]

Wittgenstein talks in a similar way, at once developing his notion of imageless thinking and repudiating the very different presuppositions of the *Tractatus*, in his *Lectures and Conversations* (page 30), where he denies that when a Frenchman says "Il pleut" and an Englishman says "It is raining," something happens in both minds which is the real sense of "It is raining." Wittgenstein explains: "We imagine something like imagery, which is the international language.[13] Whereas in fact: (1) Thinking (or imagery) is not an accompaniment of the words as they are spoken or heard. (2) The sense in the thought 'It's raining' is not even the words *with* the accompaniment of some sort of imagery."

Against the picture theory of the *Tractatus* Wittgenstein notes that even if we were to assume that we *did* have mental images, these would still have to be interpreted, and thus would be incapable, even if available, of providing an immediate and infallible point of contact between thought and reality. Thus not only is the language of the physical not reducible to the language of the mental; the latter could not in any case give us access to the ultimate constituents of reality, any more than logic gives us access to the ultimate structure of reality.

[13] This is obviously a not very veiled criticism of Otto Neurath, who had produced, as his own contribution to the school-reform program, what he dubbed the "Viennese method," which advocated the use of pictures rather than words in order to avoid verbal misunderstandings and to contribute to the creation of an international "universal language."

## X

A new explanation of error—and Wittgenstein's later thought ranks as such—has often, in the history of philosophy, led to a research program whose aim is to create conditions under which such errors will no longer arise. So it was to be with Wittgenstein. He himself never claimed that all specifically identifiable disciplines and activities in which people engaged were separate language-games each with its own sets of rules (or grammar); it is evident that he thought things more complicated than that. Many of his followers, however, made just this mistake, supposing that each individual activity—law, history, science, logic, ethics, politics, religion—has its own special grammar or logic; that mixing the grammar of one of these with that of another leads to philosophical error; and that it is the *new* job of the philosopher—his new research program under the Wittgensteinian dispensation—to describe in detail these separate logics or grammars. In this spirit two generations of British and American philosophers came to write books with titles such as *The Vocabulary of Politics*, *The Language of Morals*, *The Logic of Moral Discourse*, *The Logic of Historical Explanation*, *The Language of Literary Criticism*, *The Language of Fiction*, *The Uses of Argument*, *The Logic of the Social Sciences*, *The Logic of the Sciences*, *The Province of Logic*, *The Language of Education*, *The Logic of Religious Language*, *Faith and Logic*, *Christian Discourse*, *The Lan-*

*guage of Christian Belief, The Logic of Colour Words,*
and so on *ad nauseam.* Any philosopher, whether well-
seasoned in his subject or a budding Ph.D., was thus
provided with a simple "research formula" whereby a
book or learned paper could be produced: "Take one of
the phrases: 'The logic of *x*,' 'The language of *x*,' or 'The
grammar of *x*,' substitute for *x* some activity or discipline such as were named above; write a treatise on the
topic so created." The facile ease with which such programs could be carried out goes far to explain the immense success of such Wittgensteinian philosophizing
—as witness to which I should mention that each of the
titles cited has decorated a book or monograph actually
published. Had Russell appreciated this aspect of the
*Investigations,* he would have better understood, although he would still have been dismayed, that "a whole
school finds important wisdom in its pages."

Still, Wittgenstein himself did not endorse, or engage in, this sort of activity. Indeed, the actual sorting
out of categories, language-games, grammatical rules, or
whatever one might wish to call them, is—even granting
that it is useful—by no means easy, as Wittgenstein well
knew, and as can be shown by a few examples. Cases
often cited in illustration of mistakes in philosophical
grammar are the confusion of a class with its elements,
a university (such as Oxford, Cambridge, London, Dur-
ham, Yale, or Santa Cruz) with the colleges that com-
prise it, or a company of soldiers with the soldiers who
form it. By what criteria does one distinguish such categories? Often it is suggested that two subject terms are
of different categories, with different applicable grammars, whenever different kinds of predicates are appro-

priate to them. For instance, one would say: "The soldiers are fat" but not "The company is fat," or "The colleges are cozy" but not "The University is cozy." Similarly, it is suggested that two subject terms are of the same category whenever the same predicates may be attached to them: "being well fed," for instance, applied both to soldiers and sailors in the American forces. It is easy, however, to show that this particular way of distinguishing language-games or categories often breaks down: both a person and his body may be emaciated although the two subjects would on the face of it be thought to be of different categories. Again, whereas 2 and 0 would be regarded in many contexts as being of the same category, the first may be used as a divisor while the second cannot. Or take the difference between electromagnetic waves, light waves, sound waves and water waves: a common-sense approach might be to put the first in one category, the second and third in another category, and the last in yet another—whereas in physics the first two are put together and the last two are put together, owing in the first case to the theory that electromagnetic and light waves are identical and in the second to the theory that sound and water waves undulate in a material medium.[14]

The underlying problem here is, of course, that while it is indeed wrong to apply inappropriate criteria to a particular subject matter, we often cannot say in advance which criteria or which categories of criteria will

[14] Several examples in this paragraph are borrowed from J. O. Wisdom's very interesting discussion in "Esotericism," *Philosophy*, October 1959, pp. 346f. See also J. J. C. Smart, "A Note on Categories," *British Journal for the Philosophy of Science*, 1953.

be appropriate or inappropriate. This too will be a matter for exploration. It is, therefore, probably wrong to ask first of some criticism whether it is appropriate to its subject matter in that it, say, satisfies some such condition as "scientific character." It may be better to take the criticism seriously on its own grounds in order the better to *discover* what categories of objections one is prepared to accept against the subject matter in question. This may well come as a surprise.

Wittgenstein, as opposed to some of his followers, avoided such difficulties at least in theory: for he stoutly maintained, as part of his attack on essentialism, that no language or language-game (any more than *any* game) possessed essential defining criteria.

## XI

At the heart of the account just given of the later philosophy of Wittgenstein lies one of the basic issues of philosophy and one of the most troublesome aspects of Wittgenstein's later thinking. I have in mind the issue of the development, refinement, change, birth and death of language-games, forms of life, grammars. Although those parts of his writings dealing with this issue are obscure, a consistent, if unsatisfactory, position is stated.

The difficulty arises from three important contentions that do not in any easy way fit together. While insisting (1) that one language-game or grammar may not judge another, Wittgenstein also (2) allows (by contrast to Kant) that our language-games and grammatical categories and concepts may change, develop, evolve. Writing of the differences among kinds of sentences, Wittgenstein states: "This multiplicity is not something fixed, given once for all; but new types of language, new language-games, as we may say, come into existence, and others become obsolete and get forgotten. (We can get a *rough* picture of this from the changes in mathematics.)" (P.I. 23) Yet he goes on to say (3) that philosophy may not intervene in this change: "Philosophy may in no way interfere with the actual use of language. . . . It leaves everything as it is" (P.I. 124), and "What has to be accepted, the given, is—so one could say—*forms of life*" (P.I., page 226).

The first and third claims are often, and understandably, taken to endorse an ideological conservatism, a peaceful coexistence of those forms of life already entrenched and recognized, a stance that in practice leaves no room for change. The second claim is often either ignored or passed over as an insignificant token concession without import.

The problem is twofold. First, if conflicting language-games or forms of life are not themselves permitted to initiate grammatical change by sitting in judgment one on the other, then how *does* such change get started? And how is it to be evaluated? Wittgenstein provides no explanation. Second, if he is willing to countenance fundamental grammatical change, why does he forbid philosophy any role in effecting it? His account is at odds with the philosophical tradition, wherein it is widely assumed that perhaps the most important way to bring about fundamental categorical change lies through rational intellectual criticism involving a clash between opposing categorical frameworks. Basic shifts in the grammars of the linguistic activities in which we engage have often in the past involved criticism of one set of categories, of one grammar, of one language-game, by another. This was true in the conceptual shifts that took place in the development of modern logic, of non-Euclidean geometry, and of relativity theory by Einstein, to mention only a few important conceptual or categorical shifts with which Wittgenstein was familiar. In line with the historical record, one of Wittgenstein's own most faithful disciples, Friedrich Waismann, in a book intended to be an introductory exposition of the principles of Wittgenstein's later philosophy, cites Einstein's analysis of simultaneity as an example of conceptual change and clarification *in which philosophy aided* scientific advance.[15]

The issues at stake here—the development and change of conceptual frameworks, the scope and limits of language-games and forms of life, decision making, rule following, the nature of philosophy—are treated throughout Wittgenstein's work. Perhaps they display themselves most illuminatingly and importantly, however, in his treatment of religion. He himself seems to have sensed this. Commenting on his later philosophy, Wittgenstein once remarked: "Its advantage is that if you believe, say, Spinoza or Kant, this interferes with what you believe in religion; but if you believe me, nothing of the sort." [16] Nor have Wittgenstein's critics overlooked the significance of this part of his philosophy. Ernest Gellner's attack is representative in focusing on

[15] Waismann, *op. cit.*, pp. 11–14.
[16] Reported in W. D. Hudson, *Ludwig Wittgenstein* (Richmond: John Knox Press, 1968), p. 67. See also G. E. M. Anscombe, "What Wittgenstein Really Said," *The Tablet*, April 17, 1954.

religion. "By destroying philosophy," he states, Wittgenstein "made room for faith. . . . religious believers can find in Wittgensteinianism not merely a device for ruling out philosophic criticism, they can find in it a positive validation of their belief." [17]

Gellner's remarks are exaggerated but not unwarranted. Wittgenstein (as opposed to some of his disciples) neither provided a "positive validation" for religious belief nor ruled out criticism of religious grammars or forms of life. What he *did* do was to state that the latter was not the job of a philosopher *quâ philosopher*. In limiting the philosopher to the *description* of various categories or frameworks, Wittgenstein did indeed depart from that part of the philosophical tradition associated with such names as Plato, Spinoza, Hume, Kant, and—among Wittgenstein's contemporaries—Russell. All these thinkers stressed the need for the philosopher to undertake radical criticism of fundamental categories and even spoke at times as if this were his main role. Allowing that the tradition might be bad, one still fails to see the point of Wittgenstein's artificial construction of "the philosopher quâ philosopher." Yet, while not denying either that forms of life embodying various religions pass in and out of existence or that they might be criticized, Wittgenstein forbade the philosopher to try to effect such changes *quâ* philosopher. The distinction is silly: one does not don a certain sort of cap to make a philosophical utterance—nor does one doff it to undo one!

If Wittgenstein's approach to religion was not,

then, that of a critic, it was hardly that of a defender either. He made it quite clear that he neither supported traditional religious doctrines nor in many cases even understood what they could mean. "Suppose," he suggested, "someone said: 'What do you believe, Wittgenstein? Are you a sceptic? Do you know whether you will survive death?' I would really, this is a fact, say 'I can't say. I don't know,' because I haven't any clear idea what I'm saying when I'm saying 'I don't cease to exist,' etc." [18] Again, he remarked that although he could understand the conception of God as it involved awareness of one's sin and guilt, he could not understand the conception of a Creator. [19]

In the *Investigations*, as in other of his writings, he quite self-consciously adopted toward religion and other forms of life which were puzzling to him the role of an anthropologist or "explorer into an unknown country with a language quite strange to you" (P.I. 206-8) [20] and posed the possibility that although the people in that country had evolved a language and engaged in "the usual human activities . . . when we try to learn their language we find it impossible" (P.I. 207). What he says of such a tribe might be remarked of any number of contemporary forms of Christianity: "There is no regular connection between what they say, the sounds

[18] *Lectures and Conversations,* p. 70.
[19] Norman Malcolm, *op. cit.,* pp. 70-71.
[20] See his "Bemerkungen über Frazers *The Golden Bough,*" *Synthèse,* 1967, pp. 233-45, and Ludwig Wittgenstein, *Lectures and Conversations, op. cit.* See also Norman Rudich and Manfred Stassen, "Wittgenstein's Implied Anthropology: Remarks on Wittgenstein's Notes on Frazer," *History and Theory,* 1971, pp. 84-89.

they make, and their actions; but still the sounds are not superfluous."

Even where the language is understood, Wittgenstein allows for mutual incomprehension. "One human being can be a complete enigma to another," he observes. "We learn this when we come into a strange country with entirely strange traditions; and, what is more, even given a mastery of the country's language. We do not *understand* the people. (And not because of not knowing what they are saying to themselves.) We cannot find our feet with them." (P.I. ii, page 223). Of his close friends and students Smythies and Anscombe, both of whom had become Roman Catholics, he remarked to Malcolm: "I could not possibly bring myself to believe all the things that they believe." Malcolm adds: "I think that in this remark he was not disparaging their belief. It was rather an observation about his own capacity." [21]

Such remarks about religion as appear in his principal writings are allusive and indirect. To find a direct application of his ideas to religion, one must study his three lectures on religion in *Lectures and Conversations* and his brief critical remarks on Frazer's great work *The Golden Bough*. In both these places Wittgenstein cautions, with specific examples, against the error of approaching an alien form of life, whether primitive society or religion, with the canons of one's own society and one's own unexamined criteria of rationality and scientific respectability. Such a course is bound to lead to a misunderstanding of the alien grammar, however coherent it might be. Such an encounter must keep in focus one's own criteria of rationality as well as probing

[21] Malcolm, *op. cit.*, p. 72.

the criteria of rationality embodied in the alien form of life. If someone should charge that "Wittgenstein is trying to undermine reason," he would, he avows, reply: "This wouldn't be false"! [22] Nor would it be the first time, for his rejection of the *Tractatus*, although hardly an attempt to undermine reason, certainly battered one important *theory of rationality*.

One may easily miss the entire point of religious discourse, Wittgenstein warns, if one fails to consider that all the key terms involved—"believe," "contradict," "understand," "opinion," "error," "evidence," "prediction"—are being used outside what is for the investigator their *normal* use in nonreligious grammar. Those who participate in religious forms of life, Wittgenstein maintains, are frequently in the grip of a kind of picture; for instance, that of the rewards and punishments connected with the Last Judgment. Yet one would seriously distort one's understanding of the grammar of this form of life were one to say, "These people rigorously hold the opinion (or view) that there is a Last Judgment." [23] For it is no "opinion" of the sort that is used in nonreligious discourse, subject to usual canons of evidence, testability and high probability—which is why words like "dogma" and "faith" are likely to be used instead of "hypothesis" or "opinion."

In criticism of Wittgenstein it may well be urged that while some religious believers do use their key words in such an extranormal sense, there have been and still are many believers who hold, or claim to hold, their religious beliefs as sorts of hypotheses, subject to eviden-

[22] *Lectures and Conversations*, p. 64.
[23] *Ibid.*, p. 56.

tial support and canons of scientific testability. Wittgenstein is well aware that such persons exist, but finds them ludicrous. Such a believer, he says, "I would definitely call unreasonable. I would say, if this is religious belief, then it's all superstition. But I would ridicule it, not by saying it is based on insufficient evidence. . . . You can say: this man is ridiculous because he believes, and bases it on weak reasons." [24]

At this point Wittgenstein is not even consistent. For is that category of believers who, at least from a "normal" point of view, *misuse* scientific canons not to be allowed to do just that if that is part of *their own form of life?* And if not, is this not after all *philosophical* interference in a possible form of life? It could be rash indeed to attribute such a form of life to self-deception, even assuming that that were an unproblematic concept, for as Wittgenstein himself admonishes: "These statements would not differ just in respect to what they are about. Entirely different connections would make them into religious beliefs, and there can easily be imagined transitions where we wouldn't know for our life whether to call them religious beliefs or scientific beliefs." [25]

This weakness in Wittgenstein's treatment of religion, while submerged in his three lectures on religion, comes strongly to the surface in his brief treatment of Frazer's *Golden Bough*. While Wittgenstein is sensibly concerned to object to the snobbish assumption that "superior" nineteenth-century European cultural canons could evaluate, criticize, analyze the many religions that Frazer treated, Wittgenstein has neither evidence nor

[24] *Ibid.*, p. 59.
[25] *Ibid.*, p. 58.

satisfactory theory to counter, except in a wholly *a priori* manner, the mine of facts and connections on which Frazer draws to link a religion's *opinions* with its *rituals*.

Dismissing Frazer's explanation of rituals in terms of erroneous beliefs, opinions, and interpretations of nature, Wittgenstein coolly sets down an alternative account lacking any supporting evidence. Religious customs are, he proclaims, instinctual responses to an inner need for release and satisfaction, unconscious and with no other purpose. "When I am angry about something," he explains, "I sometimes beat on the ground or against a tree with my cane. But I do not, for that matter, believe that the earth is guilty or that beating is of any help. 'I ventilate my anger.' *And all rites are of this sort.* Such actions could be called instinctual." [26]

Even when he is being facile, as he is here, Wittgenstein is fascinating and, if unwittingly, speaks to the point. For how would an anthropologist or psychologist interpret that ritual for releasing tension that Wittgenstein adopted in the early 1920s after losing his precious rod and refusing to answer the call of his dream? Could he not wonder whether that beating of the feminine earth and the masculine tree with the phallic bamboo cane might not have something to do with some unanalyzed picture or interpretation of the world formed by a small boy growing up in the Palais Wittgenstein in the 1890s, trying to play his games among six older, bigger, and brilliantly talented children in a home whose very walls—as those who were there report—trembled when old Karl Wittgenstein strode through the front portal

[26] Ludwig Wittgenstein, "Bemerkungen über Frazers . . . ," *Synthèse*, 1967, p. 245. My italics.

and mounted up the crimson staircase? Had young Ludwig examined more closely the tree that he beat with his bamboo cane, he might even have looked up to find a golden bough.

Such speculation is also a form of life—and Wittgenstein acknowledged Freud as "my teacher."


## XII

In his last years, despite his growing physical weakness and his almost constant depression, there remained around Wittgenstein in Cambridge a group of brilliant and energetic students. No other philosopher of the past two centuries had formed a school so devoted, so talented, so responsible, or so loyal. Or so bullied: Wittgenstein tyrannized his friends and disciples, played off one against another, made cruel fun of their talents. Yet somehow he was able to preserve their loyalty without cultivating their affection.

In the autumn of 1949, shortly after a summer's visit to his former student Norman Malcolm at Cornell University, Wittgenstein learned that he was dying of cancer. Without letting his family know of his illness, he gathered together his disciples and executors-to-be and put his papers and affairs in order as best he could. That he wished some of his writings, especially his still uncompleted *Philosophical Investigations*, to be published is clear; that he ever expected they would be is not. He could not possibly have imagined the reception they would receive.

At Christmas 1949 he returned one final time to Vienna to be with his family and friends, to talk, to make music with Koder and Postl again, and to wait with Mining as she died of cancer. Not long after her death in February 1950 he left Vienna forever. Most of the rest of the year he spent in England, but that autumn he went again briefly to his hut in Norway and in a moment of optimism considered settling there. In February 1951, growing weaker, he moved into his doctor's house in Cambridge, where he died on April 29.

Throughout this time his disciples saw him regularly, and they continued to discuss philosophy until a few days before his death. He was, about himself, as lighthearted as he could be, but for the most part he maintained gloom about his written work, expressing to his friends the sort of pessimism he had already set down in the Preface to the *Investigations*: "I should have liked to produce a good book. This has not come about, but the time is past in which I could improve it. . . . These remarks . . . I make . . . public with doubtful feelings. It is not impossible that it should fall to the lot of this work, in its poverty and in the darkness of this time, to bring light into one brain or another—but, of course, it is not likely. . . . I should not like my writing to spare other people the trouble of thinking. But, if possible, to stimulate someone to thoughts of his own."

# EPILOGUE

Wittgenstein is so famous for his knack of teaching by catching one off guard that his technique has, misleadingly, been compared to that of a Zen master. Certainly he took me by surprise, for prior to my encounter with his old elementary school pupils I had had no intention of writing a book about him. No one who has read this brief study will doubt my respect for Ludwig Wittgenstein. Yet it would be wrong to part from the reader without cautioning him that this study has not been written by a disciple: I reject the main tenets of his early and later work. Should it be said that his significance lies not in any tenets but in a new style or method of philosophizing, I should have to confess that I consider the styles and methods of philosophical analysis advocated and practiced by Wittgenstein sometimes useful but quite overrated. This comment is only for the record; although I have criticized his views here and there in the preceding chapters, no critique or comprehensive assessment of his work has been given, nor was any such envisioned. Before one may criticize a philosopher responsibly, one has to determine quite precisely what his problems were and what he had to say about them. With Wittgenstein, this is still far from easy; and all too many writers, both defenders and critics, have already used his work as a kind of Rorschach blot for their own predilections.

I hope that I have not added to their number, but have, rather, encouraged someone or other to pursue some of the leads about his life and work that I have mentioned, and thereby come to a clearer understanding of him.

In any case, the progress of Wittgenstein scholarship in recent years gives some hope that the possibility of the sort of exegetical projection that has gone on since his death is nearing its end. To mention two examples, the demonstration during the past decade that the *Tractatus* is concerned primarily with logical questions and only very peripherally with epistemology has corrected a forty-year-old misreading. One may wonder how the philosophy of the past half century would have differed had that radical misinterpretation never taken place. Again, the publication of Wittgenstein's correspondence with Paul Engelmann and Ludwig von Ficker has brought into proper highlight his view of the "unwritten but more important" half of the *Tractatus*, dealing with the ethical and "the mystical"—showing more dramatically than any exegesis how far Wittgenstein was removed from logical positivism, a movement which he is still occasionally, and ridiculously, credited with having fathered.

Although Wittgenstein published only one brief philosophical book during his lifetime, and one tiny philosophical paper that he repudiated almost as soon as he had posted it to the printer, he wrote voluminously. This work, much of which has been preserved, is being published posthumously by his literary executors. Perhaps another decade or more will pass before all his work—including his remarkable correspondence—has been published, and made available in English as well as German. I mention the correspondence because so little of it has been printed, despite the vivid sense not only of the man but also of the pace and atmosphere of philosophical dialogue and humane concern that some of it conveys.

Also needed are some ambitious works in biography and intellectual history—not simply more memoirs—both from those who knew him intimately in his later years and have cared faithfully for his literary estate and those quite outside this circle of philosophers. Both kinds of biography, to be satisfactory, will have to wait on two conditions: first, the eventual accessibility—together with permission to publish—of the total corpus of the man's work and related papers; and second, the reconstruction and restoration of the most important links between Anglo-American and Austro-German philosophical traditions, links sundered by two world wars.

# ADDENDUM

回 回 回

The following brief account sets down what is known about Wittgenstein's descent. As mentioned at the beginning of the book, he was partly Jewish although this was not widely known outside the family.

When, in 1969, I mentioned his Jewish background to one of his closest surviving Viennese friends, a friend also of the family, I was assured that it was preposterous to think of Wittgenstein as Jewish, even though it was *possible* that his paternal grandmother, Fanni Figdor, was partly so. In fact, Wittgenstein went to some lengths to conceal his Jewish connections: he pleaded with a cousin living in England not under any circumstances to reveal his descent; and on his death several important obituaries, including that in *The Times* of London, stated that he was descended from the princely German family of Sayn-Wittgenstein. His only Jewish friend seems to have been the interior decorator Paul Engelmann, whose acquaintance he made while on army duty in Olmütz during the First World War.

Only since Wittgenstein's death has it become customary for biographical accounts, following that of Georg Henrik von Wright, to mention the Jewish descent, the usual account now being that he was three-quarters Jewish. This account is probably, but by no means certainly, true. Within the family itself there exist sharp divisions of opinion, some of its members claiming that both his paternal grandfather and his paternal grandmother had converted from Judaism, whereas other members stoutly maintain that his grandfather, Hermann Christian Wittgenstein, was a Gentile, the illegitimate offspring of some member of the Sayn-Wittgenstein family. To add to the confusion, some members of the Sayn-Wittgenstein family have on occasion indicated that they are related to Ludwig Wittgenstein's family. The Nazis, unable to establish the origins of the Wittgensteins of Vienna, eventually classified them as *Mischlinge* (non-Jewish but of "mixed Jewish blood") under the Nuremberg laws. Thus the property and persons of those members of the family—such as Wittgenstein's sister Hermine (Mining)—that remained within the Reich during the Second World War were unharmed. During the war, some of Wittgenstein's nephews served in the German army, others in the American army.

The truth of the matter appears to be something like this. In 1935 a family tree prepared by a source outside the family was deposited in the Vienna City Archives. According to this account, which the Nazis later used, Hermann Christian Wittgenstein was the son of a certain Hirsch Wittgenstein, a Jew of Bielefeld. A thorough search of the Bielefeld records, however, gave no evidence to connect Hirsch Wittgenstein with Hermann Christian Wittgenstein; indeed, the Nazis were unable to prove any Jewish connection in the descent of Hermann Christian Wittgenstein himself, although his wife was demonstrably Jewish, just as the wife of their son, Karl Wittgenstein, was demonstrably half-Jewish.

Another family tree, however, prepared in Jerusalem since the war, reports that Hermann Christian Wittgenstein was the son of Moses Meier Wittgenstein, Jew of Korbach, and the grandson of Moses Meier, Jew of Laasphe and Korbach. Although the records of the Jewish community in Korbach were destroyed when the SS burned the Korbach synagogue in November 1938, family tradition, comments in the diary of Hermine Wittgenstein, and significant facts—such as that the Wittgenstein family in Vienna possess portraits of Moses Meier and his wife Brendel Simon—suggest that this line of descent is correct.

If so, Ludwig Wittgenstein was indeed three-quarters Jewish, the family name having been changed from Meier to Wittgenstein in 1808 when Napoleonic decrees required that Jews adopt a surname. By the mid-1830s, almost all members of the family had converted to the Protestant religion. The history of the Meier-Wittgenstein family, in Korbach and Bielefeld, in Berlin, Leipzig, and Vienna, from their first appearance in European history toward the end of the eighteenth century until the present day, is an extraordinary—and complicated—story of remarkable talent, energy and success which well deserves study in its own right.[1]

[1] My sources for the above account are, apart from conversations with members and friends of the family, the following: (a) Wiener Stadtarchiv Ahnentafel, 1935; (b) Jerusalem Ahnentafel, 1961; (c) Wittgenstein family Ahnentafel, required by Nazis, 1938, in possession of the family; (d) *Synagogen Buch der Jüdischen Gemeinde zu Bielefeld*, by J. Posner, Staatsarchiv Detmold and Stadtarchiv Bielefeld; (e) *Kirchenbücher der Neustädter Marienkirche, ev. A.B.*, in Ev. Landeskirchenamt Bielefeld; (f) gravestones in the Jewish Cemetery of Korbach; (g) *Ein- und Auswanderung Bielefeld 1763–1874*, Stadtarchiv Bielefeld; (h) List of inhabitants of Bielefeld in 1828, Stadtarchiv Bielefeld; (i) Lutheran Church records in Vienna; (j) "Aus der Geschichte der Juden in Waldeck: Jakob Wittgenstein," in *Zeitschrift für Geschichte, Literatur, Kunst und Bibliographie*, Preßburg, January-February 1935, Volume 5, 6, pages 4–8; (k) *Korbach, die Geschichte einer deutschen Stadt*, by W. Medding, Korbach Stadtarchiv; (l) Gütersloh Liste, 1808.

# BIBLIOGRAPHY

𝕡 𝕡 𝕡

*Works by Wittgenstein:*

*Notebooks 1914–16*, ed. G. E. M. Anscombe and G. H. von Wright. New York: Barnes & Noble, 1961.

*Tractatus Logico-Philosophicus*, new English translation by D. F. Pears and B. F. McGuinness. London: Routledge & Kegan Paul, 1961.

*Wörterbuch für Volksschulen*. Vienna: Hölder-Pichler-Tempsky, 1926.

"Some Remarks on Logical Form," *Proceedings of the Aristotelian Society, Supplementary Volume*, 1929.

"A Lecture on Ethics" (1930), *The Philosophical Review*, 1965.

*Philosophische Bemerkungen* (1930), ed. Rush Rhees. Oxford: Basil Blackwell, 1965).

*Philosophische Grammatik* (1932), ed. Rush Rhees. Oxford: Basil Blackwell, 1969).

"Bemerkungen über Frazers *The Golden Bough*" (1931 and later), ed. Rush Rhees, *Synthèse*, 1967.

"Letter to the Editor," *Mind*, 1933.

*The Blue and Brown Books* (1933–35), ed. Rush Rhees. Oxford: Basil Blackwell, 1969.

*Remarks on the Foundation of Mathematics* (1937–44), ed. G. H. von Wright, R. Rhees, and G. E. M. Anscombe. Oxford: Basil Blackwell, 1967.

*Lectures and Conversations on Aesthetics, Psychology and Religious Belief* (1938), ed. Cyril Barrett. Oxford: Basil Blackwell, 1966.

*Philosophical Investigations* (1945 and 1949), ed. G. E. M. Anscombe and R. Rhees. Oxford: Basil Blackwell, 1967.

*Zettel* (1945–48), ed. G. E. M. Anscombe and G. H. von Wright. Oxford: Basil Blackwell, 1967).

*On Certainty* (1950–51), ed. G. E. M. Anscombe and G. H. von Wright. Oxford: Basil Blackwell, 1969).

For a guide to the vast secondary literature on Wittgenstein, the reader is directed to the footnotes to this book and also to the excellent long bibliography in K. T. Fann, *Wittgenstein's Conception of Philosophy* (Berkeley: University of California Press, 1969).

# INDEX